Sacred Boundaries:

Six ways to heal and step into your power

Caroline Gaskin

Contents

Part One: Sacred Boundaries

Boundaries: Where it All Began

"I have a hard time protecting my boundaries..."

"I find it exhausting....because my heart wants to just give..."

"I just want to make everyone happy, even before me...."

"Every time....it feels like I should just help...."

Does this sound like you? Well, don't worry, you are not alone! Living by your boundaries can be really hard for a spiritually minded person — but it is one of the most important things you can do for yourself, and for your empathic gifts.

Perhaps you are early on in your journey. Maybe you're a spiritual seeker just awakening, eager to learn more about spirituality and all it can bring your life. You're awakening and transforming and drawn to crystals, angels, spirit guides, herbalism, psychics, chakras, and seeing signs and patterns all around you. Perhaps you're cautious who to share these new interests with and keep them largely to yourself and the social media groups you join for fear of what friends and

4

family may say. What you are learning is changing how you see the world. If this is you, living by healthy boundaries is something that will become increasing important as your journey evolves. These boundaries will help you live authentically without fear, and I wish I'd known that and worked on them early in my own journey.

Maybe you resonate with being an Earth Angel, connected with the energies around you and your intuition. You're reading all the books, doing your courses, learning more all the time. You're developing a deep trust in yourself, your higher self, your spirit guides and you're connecting with their messages and guidance. You need your healthy boundaries to help you step into your full power. Your healthy boundaries will, amongst other things, protect your energy and give you balance, and the healing you undertake while working on boundaries will emphasise your own gifts and magic even further.

Or perhaps you're a light worker, working with spirit full time, using your connections, your compassion and energy to help others live their best life. You're following your purpose and walking the guided path presented to you. Healthy boundaries help you to be your best self to help others. Your boundaries, amongst other things, help your professional relationship with clients, give you the energy to work your purpose, and the balance to feed yourself. With boundaries in place, you are empowered and don't face issues like drain and overwhelm; your purpose and path are clear.

Whatever stage of your spiritual journey (and throughout the book I will just use the generalised term — spiritually minded people) Sacred Boundaries and this work is for you.

As I learnt ….

It is a beautiful summer morning. I'm 38 years old, standing on the side of a major A road, 100 miles from home. I was looking at my car wondering and trying to piece together what just happened. The side of the car is all smashed up and looks like it met with an angry Wolverine! There's hardly any front left-hand side wing, doors don't look like doors should, the handles have been ripped off. It's a mess - and in fact in a matter of days I will be told that it turns out to be a write-off!

I sense some pain, but I don't properly feel it. I'm bleeding, but I don't recognise the sensation. Because part of me is there on the side of the road silently falling to pieces - the most vulnerable, scared and lost I have ever felt; and part of me is in my *I have to* mode and is already brushing this whole incident off to go about my day ahead.

There are two very clear, very distinct voices in my head. One chastising myself: *"You stupid cow!! How and why did you think you could drive today? Look at what you ev'done!"* and the second - screaming even louder — *"You need to get to that meeting! Don't let them down."*

Now, rest assured that no one other than myself put the pressure on me to drive that day. You see when I had that accident, I had a stent fitted in one of my kidneys. I'd just had one emergency surgery and was waiting for a second operation. I was on strong, hospital prescription painkillers, and the person I was meeting knew only some of my situation (because I had heavily played it down of course), and still insisted we postpone. But not wanting to show weakness; not wanting to be anything less than these people thought I should be or was (an expectation of course set only in my own head); and not wanting to not be the happy, just fine, positive, people-pleasing self I was, I said, *"I'm fine, I'd love to come"*.

So, there I am, on the side of the road- bleeding, in pain, and in shock. I had fallen asleep at the wheel of my car whilst in the fast lane and drifted into the side of a lorry (who hadn't even seen little me), having taken painkillers to even get out of bed that morning. But I'm getting back into the car, I'm wiping the blood off my forehead, I'm putting some extra make-up on, popping another painkiller, and with a quick spritz of perfume I'm ready. The engine starts, the car has to be driven with me constantly turning the steering wheel 45 degrees to the left to stay in a straight line, but I'm moving. In my head I repeat *"It's fine, I'm great, just smile, keep going."*

I get to my destination, and I text my husband to say I've arrived. Bit of a rough journey I tell him, but all ok. I'll fill him in on the details later. Because why worry him when there's nothing he can do? I never want to cause anyone any concern. I head to my meeting with a very fake, smile on my face and my best calm and enthusiastic head on for my day ahead.

Am I in shock? Am I delusional? I think in that moment I'm both of those. There's a mix of adrenaline, fear and shock just racing through me for the next few hours. There's two of me that day and in the weeks to come. One of me striding forward, like everything is okay, and one of me a few steps behind, in a shadow: shaking, crying, ashamed, scared, and unable to bear being seen. But she's there — and she's very, very real.

One thing I remember from the minutes, or moments, before I fell asleep was that I had prayed to Archangel Michael and my spirit guides to just get me through the day, to get me home that night, and to make it all okay. When I look back now, I think that these are the most interesting choice of words. I could have asked for my drive to be a safe one or my meeting to be successful — but to get me home and to make "it" all okay is really what they did. Perhaps not in the way I had literally meant in that moment of prayer, but in the way that I needed most.

The good thing about this whole story is that the accident bought me to where I am today. I write this full of gratitude for that day. It is from that incident that I found, healed and embraced the vulnerable girl hidden deep within me. I chose to love her and step into my spiritual gifts to the full. Because that night, and in the days afterwards, when I eventually physically collapsed and broke down in tears- shaking, my body and brain just trying to make sense of what had happened- I went into a deep healing process.

It took months of work to come to realisation that ignoring my own boundaries was at the core of many issues. It hadn't only been at the core of the car accident; it was why I was living deep in the spiritual closet (imagine Narnia). It was why I sometimes cried about friendships and my feelings of not fitting in. It was why I was getting deeper into debt. Although I had overcome many anxieties in my life, I was shying away from other things that were affecting me. I re-evaluated everything during this time. I started to understand the importance of being vulnerable and living wholly as my spiritual and empathic self. I came to understand the need for boundaries, and I live by them. I was largely healed by these boundaries and the work to acknowledge and communicate them.

While my spiritual courses and the development work I had loved, and was so inspired by, all showed me that looking after myself was essential, I was wrapped up in people-pleasing and toxic positivity. Everything was wonderful while I fixed other people. I felt that I just needed to be totally focused on love and light.

But that isn't the human experience we are here for.

Catalyst for change

Sometimes it takes something to shake you to your very core. Something that you gain a different perspective and outlook from, and for me it was that day. One day, one moment. From all the healing work that followed, I took my spiritual beliefs and work public (because if my angels hadn't saved me that day - then I wouldn't be typing this now). But, more importantly, I stopped automatically saying yes, and I started living from an authentic heartfelt space, putting me and my care first.

I asked people in the spiritual community who are on their spiritual journey- sensitive people, intuitives, healers, earth angels, light workers, spiritually minded people just like you and I- if they found it difficult to live by their boundaries. Almost all those I asked said at one point or another in their journey, and particularly more recently, this was a yes.

Why?

That very light inside that drives us to want to live our purpose, to make a difference, to help people and to serve can also mean we find it difficult to have healthy boundaries in place. We don't intend to or maybe even realise our actions, but we can forget to put ourselves and our energy first. We would rather say yes, then upset someone by saying no. We want to help and sort out all the troubles being experienced. Whether or not that is more than we can realistically do.

The strong desire to help can be such a loud call, one that can become overwhelming in itself, and spiritually minded people are very good at coming up with solutions and wanting to fix people. In fact, we often feel the need to do everything we can to fix people. That in itself can lead to codependency with the people we are helping and relying on their happiness for our own feelings of fulfilment and joy.

What we have come to live through since the start of 2020 has been, without a doubt, the strangest of times — whatever your beliefs. It has tested all of us in different ways. As people on a spiritual journey, wherever in that journey you are, it bought a shift in energy that many of us had not felt before.

Many of us had an understanding of how Mother Earth had needed our nations lockdowns and our cars and planes to stop, and from that a level of acceptance came that it was hard to explain to those not on the same journey as us. At the same time, we felt the enormity of the collective pain and fear. We felt the losses and the divides that came. It was a constant empathic rollercoaster.

The Covid-19 pandemic, for many of us, was the biggest call to rise we had received since we started our spiritual journey. We were called to help, to heal — not only people that we knew and, in our communities, but globally. And we rose. But then came the feelings of drain and overwhelm — simple, but very real reminders from the Universe that we must take care of ourselves.

The times we feel pressured to drop our boundaries are possibly when our call to serve is at its loudest — but these times are also when our boundaries are most needed.

Then we had to readjust to everyday life in a slightly different world to the one we knew before. But it didn't stop there. Then came issues with our jobs and income, a collective worldwide fear that lingered from the pandemic, and then the awful announcement that a war was going on in Ukraine.

We don't know if we will ever go back to the world as we knew it before. We may not want to. As we try to move forward, we adjust to the energy shifts that we experienced throughout these past few years, as well as the adjustments the future unfolding will need us to continue to make. We process and heal. Boundaries are a vital part of that healing.

After my accident I read the more traditional, psychology style books around boundaries, and their ways and thinking helped me, but never 100%. I always slipped back into old patterns and ways, or just made excuses to have a boundary line of sorts in place, but it wasn't a healthy, honest one. I didn't see that this deep spiritual healing side would help my boundaries at first. However, the way I see it now is that the pain, hurt, drain, and feelings of confusion and overwhelm that a lack of boundaries can bring all need healing. We need to work on is what lies underneath the feelings of fear that comes with boundaries. This work is more than learning to say no. It goes back to our childhood, our ancestors, lifetimes lived before this one, and a deep forgiveness for all that has been. This work is essential to our wellbeing, our spiritual health and embracing who we truly are.

Embracing the spiritual and sensitive people we are, with all the gifts that brings us, and doing the healing work brings us to the point of being our best, empowered self. We gain confidence, we learn to speak our truth, and we step into our power.

Boundaries have been at the very core of my healing. Learning the ability to just be me and to say no wasn't easy. Lifting the burden of the needs and expectations of others from my own shoulders was challenging. But all the work and reflection bought me a new perspective and a life I am in control of, where I am truly happier living.

As spiritually minded people, we have to learn that boundaries are key to all we are here for. Our purpose, our work, the light and healing we offer the world is strongest when we are at our best - and boundaries are, for me and many others, are where that all begins.

I understand that any healing work we undertake can seem insurmountable at the start. It can be incredibly daunting and feel like this is too much. I want to reassure you that what follows in these pages is a gentle, transformative process, where you will be supported by your gifts and spiritual tools. But I also want to be honest with you that this isn't a one-off process, and — like any healing — isn't without its emotional times. In practice, boundaries can be hard. In day-to-day life we can waiver and wobble at times. Like an onion, it comes in layers, and we just have to keep going and evolving as we grow, maybe with the odd tear or two.

Some people disappeared from my life during this process. It wasn't easy. In fact, I will keep it very honest with you, it was hard. At times it was hard enough that I thought about burying my feelings deep, sticking my head in the sand and just getting on with life. But I needed to do this work. The universe had shown me that this was how it needed to be. The people that did leave my circle of friends I now see we're not really friends, or right for me to have around me. I noticed that when I stopped making an effort, or being too fully available, these 'friendships 'ended. But that was because it was never two-sided. It was always based more on me- my time and my energy.

The healings I detail in this book made a big difference to my boundaries, and so many aspects of who I am and how I live now. There is always more work I can do; I don't believe I am perfectly living by my healthy boundaries all of the time. I waiver like we all will. But I see the progress that has been made. So, see this book as your starting point. At the end of the book, we will close with a ritual to honour how far you have come on this journey.

Throughout the book you will find stories from my own experiences, rituals, practices and journalling prompts. I've found journalling to be a hugely healing practice. Getting my thoughts and words out and understanding where my feelings came from, helped me to see how experiences showed themselves in my day-to-day life. Even taking those pages and burning them helped me release, and surrender. This supported me in saying goodbye to the old and welcoming in the new. If you don't like journalling with pen and paper, then you could go for a walk or sit quietly and just talk it all out. Record it if you can and just speak your thoughts and feelings out. If you are going to put pen to paper, now is the time to find a lovely journal, perhaps one with images that are bright and colourful, or will simply make you feel warm and smile when you see it.

I also want to invite you to join me in an online community of fellow readers who have either been through or are going through their own journey to have sacred boundaries in their lives. You are not alone in this work. Find out more at **_www.sacredboundaries.co.uk_**. Surrounding ourselves with people who will share, understand and support our journey only makes our healing and the work we're doing easier. Having a community and a cheer squad behind us is everything to me — and I can't wait to meet you!

And finally — before we begin — take three deep breaths, place both hands, one on top of the other, on your heart space and affirm to yourself "*I am worthy of setting sacred boundaries for my life.*"

Sacred = regarded as too valuable to be interfered with, extremely important and deserving respect.

Boundaries = the limit of what someone considers to be acceptable behaviour.

Spirituality and Boundaries

I started my spiritual journey 20 years ago when I was drawn to crystals, Feng Shui, and writing letters to the universe to let it know what I wanted for my life (I later came to know this as manifesting)! There were points where I did no practice at all, in fact years went by at one point.

In 2016 a series of synchronicities lead me to the work of Kyle Gray, and shortly after I joined his 'Angel Team' development course. There I met like-minded people, all learning like I was and sharing our experiences. It was wonderful. I was keen to explore more. I signed up for more courses, read books, excited by learning more with each lesson or page turn. I was this intuitive, empathic person that was spoken about! Things started to fall into place, behaviours and characteristics I had I started to understand and began to seem clearer for me in many ways. All of a sudden it clicked as to why I hated crowds, was never someone who could handle drinking alcohol, was so raw with emotion at times, cried at charity adverts on television, and said yes, a lot when I really didn't want or mean to! My fears started to add up to — I was hypersensitive to the world and what was going on, and the bad things scared me. At times I was driven to hit refresh on the internet news pages or not turn way from the 24-hour live streams because my fears of what was happening in the world overwhelmed me.

I decided I could change these behaviours. What I was

learning about my spiritual side made want to embrace my empathy in a positive way. Understanding my empathic traits now meant I wasn't scared to ask for help. My spiritual studies gave me some coping mechanisms and the confidence to explore traditional therapies and CBT alongside.

Even though all this work brought me so much joy and happiness and I could feel the change in me, I was firmly in the spiritual closet away from the groups and safe online spaces I had found. Narnia deep in it in fact! I had all these amazing friendships growing in various groups but the people in my 'normal' life had no idea about that side of me. And they were not going to get a look! What would they think of me?

Imagine living your life as two people (although you might not have to because you may well do the same). One person is who you really are deep down, spiritual, connected, changing and growing; so excited for this life that is unfolding! And the second person is the one you show the world and that the people around you know and have come to rely on being a certain way. That second person within me quite quickly felt deflated. Chained-in almost. However, she remained the person a lot of people could see.

The shift

In 2019 I found myself invited to be on a stage in London by Kyle Gray with seven other ladies, in front of a room of wonderful people all about to experience Kyle's angel teachings while we supported him. I was empowered and lifted from the moment of the invite to the day itself. We danced and shared stories, and the weekend was filled with amazing connections and energy. After the accident, I had experienced a lot of self-healing work. To now have this wonderful weekend meant I cried with joy all the way home. I had been broken open and filled with love by my experiences and the people I'd met and shared it all with. I had to allow myself to be my full authentic self all of the time!

Many of us, especially spiritually minded people, have been taught over the generations to give and give, without asking for anything or taking anything for ourselves. We are likely living with soul contracts where we are these over-giving people, and these binding agreements may mean we live lifetime after lifetime putting other people before ourselves. But we can change this. Creating boundaries, saying no, and asking the world for what you need makes space for the big **yes** to come into your life. Living by our boundaries isn't just about saying no, it's about saying yes to what feels good, what nourishes us, and what lights us up.

In his book '*Light Warrior*', one of my favourite mentors, Kyle Gray (who I credit with a lot of my most recent journey and spiritual development), says '*Whatever you do for yourself is what you offer up to the world*'.

'*A Course in Miracles*' by Helen Schucman tells us that '*When I am healed I am not healed alone*'.

For me, it's so important spiritually minded people remember these sentiments because when we look after ourselves, we really are also helping others. Our energy and what we give out influences those around us — there is a direct correlation between the two that we should always be mindful of. We should make our spiritual self-practice and self-care an important part of our everyday lives. We need to love ourselves enough to bring the balance and benefits of boundaries into our lives.

Through having and living by our boundaries, we teach others to do the same. We pass on our way of being and by doing so encourage others to do the same. What an amazing ripple effect it is to put that out into the world!

Why can boundaries be difficult for spiritually minded people?

Spiritually minded people feel the emotions of others and pick up on the vibrations around us. Positive energy charges and empowers us, but negative energy can leave us feeling low, tired and emotional. I believe these and our other traits are gifts we are blessed to understand and nurture. Yet we need to look after our boundaries to look after ourselves, and ultimately enhance our gifts and lives. We are unique individuals with unique needs — and we shouldn't feel guilty for that.

As spiritually minded people, we may experience a number of spiritual gifts. What these are, how much we use and connect with these gifts will be up to you and personal for everyone. These gifts give us a different insight into day-to-day life. They really are our superpowers! By embracing them and working to protect them we can grow and develop spiritually. Living as spiritually minded people can be difficult at times but embracing our gifts and living by our healthy boundaries is empowering.

Often, we are called to explore and discover who we truly are and live this life as our authentic self. I know that it can be difficult and may seem impossible in fact to show your true identity out in the world. Many spiritually minded people, just like me, start off in the spiritual closet and there is a fear about showing the world who we are and our beliefs. Boundaries help us reveal ourselves by giving us the ability to speak our truth.

We are called to live our purpose on this earth, whatever we discover that to be. For me this journey took me to take my spiritual coaching, readings and healing out into the local community. Healthy boundaries allow us to carry out this work without being drained or overwhelmed.

We are compassionate and connect with our feelings and the feelings of others. We are natural healers and nurturers. Healthy boundaries allow us to process those feelings and not be taken advantage of by the people around us.

We are deeply connected with nature and are re-energised by spending time outdoors. Our boundaries allow us the time to enhance and experience this connection.

Many spiritually minded people are connected to our intuition and our 'clairs' (different types of psychic ability that connect to our senses). We need time, space, and clear energy to enhance this connection to listen and process the messages that are coming through to us. Again, it's our boundaries that make this possible!

There is a significant difference in how we operate and use our gifts with and without boundaries in place. Ignoring our boundaries, or allowing people to cross them, has different effects on spiritually minded people than for non-spiritual people. For instance, healers will experience blocks in their own self-healing sessions. The energy flow differs. Without boundaries we can become weak, overwhelmed, feel burdened, and suffer from illness, dis-ease (a word I learnt from Louise Hay, which refers to the way our body experiences pain) and burn out.

However, with boundaries in place we are aligned, centred, we can appreciate and resonate with nature, our healing abilities flow and we are empowered by our empathic gifts. In fact, our empathic gifts can develop and strengthen when they are supported by boundaries. We can enjoy our spiritual practice and work without being overstimulated, giving, and receiving in a balanced way —and balance holds power.

Boundaries show people that we value ourselves and understand our true worth. Low self-esteem (a tendency of spiritually minded people who don't embrace their gifts), and the desire to just feel normal (whatever we consider normal to be) and fit in are both stumbling blocks when it comes to setting and living by boundaries. I would struggle in some social situations, bothered by small talk, wanting deeper connections that didn't come. But this journey showed me that I don't have to have that in every situation. For some people that connection is just at that level. Some are deeper. But having that balance bought a shift my energy needed, and an acceptance of me being me!

Boundaries can be difficult for spiritually minded people to set and live by. We are natural people-pleasers who don't want to offend, hurt or upset people, and we shy away from conflict. As people pleasers, we can feel drained by people pulling on our energy — but at the same time find it difficult and feel guilty for saying no. When we don't let people know what is and isn't acceptable behaviour to us — either consciously through our words, or subconsciously through our actions — then they will naturally conclude that we are fine with how they are treating us. Nothing tells or shows them anything different.

It can be easier to use avoidance techniques to deal with the issues caused by people crossing our boundaries. It avoids those first difficult steps laying down our boundaries. When we haven't communicated our boundaries previously, we do risk that the people around will find it strange and perhaps difficult to adjust to our new ways of being. However, we can't go on putting our needs aside. Avoidance is simply not a healthy boundary. We can't just ignore the phone forever or leave words that need saying left unsaid. Long term, those sorts of strategies bring us more problems than good.

Through no fault of our own, spiritually minded people and those who don't lay down boundaries are often taken advantage of. So, a spiritually minded person struggling with boundaries is even more likely to have expectations and demands that are more than is reasonable or fair put on them! Needy people are naturally attracted to us. If you find yourself surrounded by needy people, that is simply your empathic tendencies shining through. We provide something people need and are naturally drawn to.

One of the things that became clear to me after my accident was how and where I was being taken advantage of. When I shut down and withdrew from my world, there were people who had been in regular contact with me, mostly to share their problems, until that very point. But when I was not open and available to them on their terms, they simply disappeared.

I was someone who would listen and take on the everyone's problems and issues, and inadvertently I had given myself the role of agony aunt and general emotional dumping ground. I was the person people went to advice and guidance and was so aware of their issues, I didn't allow myself the time to have a bad day or a day when I simply couldn't listen or give advice. Taking on the weight of other people's problems and having nowhere or limited people you can share your problems with leads to a lonely place where you start to feel resentful. With no outlet and no one to turn to, I started to feel incredibly alone and isolated. As a result of what I'd created, I would feel awful and talk to myself harshly for feeling resentful! I'm sure I'm not alone in this — and it's a cycle that is hard to break. There can be a lot of negative self-talk associated with putting boundaries in place. We simply can't fix or be everything for everyone, and we definitely shouldn't hold ourselves accountable for being so or berate ourselves for not doing so.

Putting so much of our time and energy into other people is draining — both emotionally and physically. Always being available for friends, family and others can be exhausting and leave us without the energy to focus on our own needs. Fear is also a big issue when it comes to the people in our lives. Setting boundaries can be triggering. Not only do we worry about offending, upsetting and hurting people, but we fear that people will reject us when we are not always open and available to them.

Typically, we may also find we have the tendency to not share our problems in return. Or we may share them but feel like we are simply not heard. So, there isn't the balance that a healthy, supportive relationship has. Without that outlet for our problems, we can internalise and keep things to ourselves so that we do not feel like a burden to others. If you have read Louise Hay's '*You Can Heal Your Life* 'you know the effects on our health such behaviours have.

Whenever I'm suffering from any ailment, I will refer to '*You Can Heal Your Life*'. Recognising how what my body is experiencing is rooted with what I'm actually feeling helps fight and prevent dis-ease within. Being in touch with these feelings and their effects is essential as we go through our journey. Listening to our bodies tells us so much about what we need to work on and address, where we are stretching ourselves too thin, and when we need to take a step back.

We can't always be in love, light and unicorns' mode, not every thought will be a positive one. That's not the human experience anyone is here for! Accepting that can be difficult — confidently living by that can be even harder.

I believe and see that there is a sad trend becoming more apparent — toxic positivity — where people feel the pressure, especially in the spiritual community, to constantly be putting out a positive vibe and never having a negative thought. We've been told to live in this high vibration, but it can be taken too far — to the point where I've seen numerous posts in online groups where people worry that something bad will happen because they have had a negative thought or have had a bad day. This worries me! We have to be kind enough and loving enough to ourselves to not add this extra pressure to our load. We aren't perfect and we shouldn't put the undue pressure on ourselves to be so. We are enough, just as perfectly imperfect as we are!

As many of us are reminded, with the light naturally comes the dark. We will experience life the same way everyone does — with the good and the bad. This toxic positivity causes many in the spiritual community to drop, forget or simply feel unable to live with balance and boundaries when the dark moments come. It makes it more difficult to have those days where we aren't in the energetic place to hold space for others, where it is harder to honour ourselves and how we feel because the pressure is to be in 'love, light and unicorns ' mode all day, every day. But that simply isn't realistic, and we need to keep it real!

We have, and we are allowed to have, flaws and make mistakes — all people do! We need to not judge ourselves (or others) for being like that and we need to learn to accept all our traits. For one thing, these traits make us unique individuals. When we embrace our mistakes, we can benefit from the lessons and what we learn from them. We live in a world where nothing is perfect, nor will it ever be — let's embrace that!

My own toxic positivity was something I worked to overcome. Mine came from a place of feeling the need to be positive for people around me all the time and the need to live up to everything I promised to be. If I agreed to something, I had to do it — no matter whether circumstances changed, or whether I really even wanted to say yes in the first place. Alongside my always being positive outlook and "everything is great" smile! But was this me being my authentic self?

Like so many of us do, I had painted a picture in my head of what I needed to be for people, in my job, to my family, and to my friends. A lot of this was heavily influenced, rightly or wrongly, by what I felt their expectations of me were. These largely, like many other people, centred around me being as close to 'perfect '(whatever that meant) as I could be. We need to not allow ourselves to be consumed by other people's expectations. Especially when we set unrealistic expectations in our heads.

Doing this spiritual work and being of service means serving ourselves first. Serve ourselves before we serve others. Help ourselves with healthy boundaries because doing light work is not about self-sacrifice. Through serving ourselves, respecting and loving ourselves, we teach others to do the same. Through having the integrity to say no when we mean and need to say no, we help others to do the same. Living with healthy boundaries in place shows others how to do the same for themselves. Every lesson we live by we inspire others.

We are the shift; we can be the change!

Benefitting from boundaries

Boundaries are a vital step on a healing journey and using our spiritual tools — meditation, energy protection, grounding, and much more — gives us a unique and wonderful ways to work with boundaries for our highest good. Learning how to both handle the emotions that come with being an empath and how to openly discuss our needs is vital. Learning how to be present but to not soak up the energy of others is essential.

We have needs and we need space to take care of ourselves, get to know ourselves, tune into our feelings and process them. Ask yourself…. how do I feel? What do I need? When we understand what we want and need it is easier to set boundaries and to be our true, authentic self.

Ultimately, boundaries benefit everyone. We will have more

energy, more patience, and we won't feel resentful towards people. Boundaries protect us and our energy. They stop negative people and their energies draining us, stop burn out, and help us see and accept that we simply can't fix, protect, help, and heal everything.

Boundaries show that we are people who know and respect ourselves, who weed out the good relationships from the bad, who shine our light, and have the time and space to show up for the people we love. Having these boundaries in place benefits our relationships, career, home life — in fact all the corners and aspects of our lives! We are also left in a space where we are able to benefit from the spiritual laws, like the Law of Attraction. What we omit once our boundaries are in place is confidence, a healthy vibe, and what we attract back into your life will mirror that.

As a spiritually minded person, you understand that the energy we put out will help shape the energy we receive from others. It's basic Law of Attraction. Like attracts like — the energy we put out will attract an energy to us! With that understanding, please know and be reassured of one thing — dealing with people and putting boundaries into place gets easier. I can tell you that because it really did for me, and I know it will for you. When we live by heathy boundaries, our energy changes. We stop putting out the energy that people can cross those lines and drain us. We put out a strong, positive energy that attracts the respect, kindness and appreciation that the "boundaried" us shows to the world.

It's not to say that once we have boundaries life is going to be all sunshine and roses, or without any blips or dramas. What it does mean however, is that you when you have to cope with life's dramas, as your energy is coming from a strong place from the start, you will know how to best care for yourself and others through those times. And don't worry — boundaries don't mean you're going to be an ice queen or king, or a total loner who doesn't want anyone or anything around them!

Without boundaries we simply can't serve or be the spiritually minded people we are here to be. The process in the chapters that follow will support you with your own healing boundary journey. But what is a boundary?

First of all, let's just address the different types of boundaries:

Physical boundaries are all about your space and body. These are important boundaries as they let people know how it is ok to approach and interact with us physically and within our personal space.

Emotional boundaries separate our emotions from those of other people around us, and not allowing someone else's emotions to dictate or influence how we feel personally, not taking responsibility for other's feelings, or blaming other people for how we feel.

Intellectual boundaries help us communicate our thoughts, ideas and beliefs to others, while respecting that others may not share ours, and respecting that their thoughts differ from our own. It is also knowing when it's best to step away from certain conversations to ensure our own wellbeing.

Spiritual boundaries allow us to stay spiritually sovereign and rooted in our beliefs and how they support our lives. They allow us to accept and respect that there are many spiritual belief systems and that we do not all share the same faith.

Energetic boundaries are all about our energy body and auric field. It's important to have energetic boundaries to protect and keep our energy safe and our auric field free of energetic clutter.

Digital boundaries are becoming increasingly important. It's important to set boundaries around the use of digital products and social media to ensure that we are not drained by content that is harmful to our mental and physical health.

Then our boundaries fall into categories — desires, deal breakers, compromise. So, ask yourself what it is you desire when it comes to these boundaries? How do you want it to really be — what is your goal?

Then what's really firm when it comes to boundaries — what's a deal breaker for you? For me, after everything, one of my deal breakers is that if my body tells me it needs a break, it gets one — no matter what.

Then there's boundaries where we are willing to compromise

for the good of the overall situation. By compromise I don't mean giving in to someone else's viewpoint — I mean where we can have a conversation and come to a central safe point where we are both happy and feel respected. But we also know and are aware of the limits we have to that compromise. This flexibility isn't so we can have people cross our boundaries — this is so that they are healthy boundaries, which is incredibly important.

The following chapters primarily focus on spiritual, emotional and energetic boundaries, as these are often where spiritually minded people need the most support and where the healing in this book can really make a difference. From mastering these, I know the other areas will come more naturally. Only you will know what falls into your desires, deal breakers and what you're happy to compromise on. But all this together gives you the flexible, healthy, honouring yourself boundaries that will work best for you.

———————————————

So, what do boundaries look like for you?

Close your eyes. Imagine you are standing on a beach. In front of you, golden sand, further still you can hear the waves of the ocean lapping in the distance. You can feel the sun on your face and the sand crunching under your feet. This is a great place to be right now. The perfect place. You feel happy, relaxed, calm, and you stand there being your best self, shining like a bright beam of light. With a stick in your hand, you draw a line in the sand in front of where you stand from the left to the right.

That's a boundary.

On your side of the boundary all the senses, feelings, and pieces of your life that you are happy to have in your life. On the other side of that line the things that don't fit with you.

That strong boundary line in the sand is governed by you. You decide which side everything falls on — people, their behaviours, places, thoughts, stories — everything. You decide what can cross the line and come into your energetic space and be part of your life. You decide what stays on the other side.

So, standing on this beach, with your line, what you do want on your side? What do you want some distance from? What stays on the other side of the line?

Now grab your journal and make some notes on everything that came up for you during this visualisation.

When we have healthy boundaries no one, no situation, will disturb our inner serenity. We will have that inner strength, peace, and mindset to cope with life. We will be happy in our space being our authentic self.

A few things to remember about living with our boundaries in place:

- We are not being rude or selfish by setting firm boundaries,
- We are not mean for setting boundaries,
- We are entitled to set boundaries for ourselves and live by them,
- People around us may find the changes difficult to accept at first — but they will come around.

Healing as we undertake this boundary journey will dig deep, reveal what we truly need, lay down our rules for how people interact with us on an energetic level, and ultimately empower us.

I like to think of it like exercise. Our first visit to the gym in a long time is not where we are going to achieve our best results or feel the fittest we have ever felt. But we go, and we go again, and it gets easier. Our body adapts, the habit is formed, we feel better, and we are healthier.

And that's how I think of boundaries. They are one of the healthiest habits and behaviours we can put into place. They help us become the best version of ourselves — an empowered us, living our best, most authentic life.

Remember, when we say yes when we really want to say no, we are abandoning ourselves. We are not looking after ourselves. Our relationship with ourselves really is the most important relationship to look after. Truly, our spiritual practice is about how we treat ourselves, how we treat people, where we go and what we do in the world, and how we set the boundaries to allow all of that to flow.

With healthy boundaries in place, as a spiritually minded person, you can:
- find balance in your life,
- have more time and / or energy to enjoy the things you want to do and that light you up,
- benefit from your energy and auric field being clear of the drain of others,
- experience better mental health,
- live the life you want to be living,
- fully step into your gifts and power,
- feel less drained and overwhelmed.

'I am kind and loving toward others while creating clear boundaries that protect my good feeling emotions' - Gabby Bernstein.

Healing and Boundaries

"Earth Angels often have the hardest time saying "no", or honouring their own true feelings. They've been sent to blanket the earth in divine angelic love, and this can get confused in worldly relationships with saving and rescuing people from their own issues. It can be very uncomfortable to step away from helping or being there for everyone or everything, but Earth Angels really come into their own when they start practicing discernment and respect when it comes to honouring their own emotional and physical limits". - Sophie Bashford

Boundaries can be an uncomfortable mindset to get into and exist by, but I don't believe it is difficult to live with our boundaries in place. I just believe it can be uncomfortable to get used to. But how do we know whether we need stronger, healthier boundaries in our life?

Weak, unhealthy, wavering boundaries can look like always feeling like we have to be available for others at the times they want and demand of us. We may feel unbalanced or drained a lot of the time, and like we don't have time for a break or proper rest. We may also feel like we can't say no because that's selfish or it makes us feel really uncomfortable.

Over the years, my wishy washy, non-existent boundaries actually caused a lot of pain. While I was trying to go along with others, I was often giving myself anxiety attacks. My brave face was hiding a lot of inner turmoil.

On one occasion, I'd handed my notice in at a previous job. It was a hard day, with many at the company being told they were at risk of redundancy. At the same time, I knew, although my role was safe, my heart was no longer there, and I was looking to leave. 95% sure I had a new role, and feeling the shock, pain and distress colleagues were going through (in that way only an empath can), I bought handing my notice in forward. That way someone knew there was at least one more role they could potentially apply for.

But I was asked to stay. Everything inside me screamed **no, no, no**! I really wanted out. I had been bullied by a couple of people, I had come to the end of the line and my energy and health were at an all-time low. My head told me to stay firm, master that boundary line. I had said I was leaving, I needed to stand by that. But I wavered. Someone asking me to stay made me want to disappear into my usual pattern of people-pleasing behaviour. They had that expectation that I might say yes. That inner argument made me ask for a week to think about it.

Two days later and my phone was ringing time and time again for an answer (so much for giving me a week), my heart crying out for me to listening to it. My ego was going through all the fear talk about starting somewhere new. But I still knew it was a no. But actually, saying no was something

I couldn't do; I couldn't even start to have that conversation again. It had taken so much out of me the first time.

The phone rang so many times, the pressure became too much — to the point of giving me a panic attack. I knew what I was going to say, but saying it, putting the words out there, with all the risk of disappointing someone, of facing confrontation, was all too much. I ended up sick in bed for the day.

The phone still rang. Probably because I'd never had boundaries and not answered my phone while I'd been on holiday or off sick previously. So, to them, my past behaviour meant it was fine to keep calling. Sick or not. I'd always allowed that in the past and answered, never showing that I had any issue with that sort of behaviour.

So, I text to say I was still leaving. More panic and anxiety, another day in bed. When I look back now, I know it all stemmed from the fact that I couldn't enforce my boundaries — either by just politely saying no at the very start, or by being pushed to answer quicker than I'd asked for. And that's just one time something like this happened to me — there have been many, many, more.

———————————————

So where are you with your boundaries? Are you just starting on your boundary journey? Are you someone who has boundaries in place? Do you feel they waiver too much at times?

I don't doubt we have some boundaries in place already. For instance, I knew I had boundaries in place - I never leave the house without a bra, I don't let strangers touch me, and I don't allow myself to get into shouting arguments with rude, aggressive people. While these may seem silly, simple or trivial, acknowledging that you we have boundaries in place is an important first step. It shows that we have the ability to live by boundaries. I believe that sometimes we need to acknowledge what we already do to help us move forward.

Think back to the beach visualisation in the previous chapter - you drew a line in the sand. You pictured everything that went on each side of that line. So, here's a newsflash for you......You don't need to set boundaries. You already have them. You need to heal to remove the blocks to living by them.

When I dug deeper, I knew that really, I had all sorts of boundaries in place. I knew when something didn't sit with me well, when I wanted to say no, and when situations made me feel uncomfortable. I just had to do the work to become more comfortable living by them. The awareness that, yes, I could do this process, set that line, hold it firm and enforce it was a good and reassuring moment. It helped me to see that although it felt like a mountain of work was ahead of me, I could take the first step. I could start my journey. So now it's your turn...

Sit down for a few quiet and moments and ask yourself some of these questions - you may want to grab a notebook and pen and write about how each makes you feel:

- *What are your currently beliefs about boundaries?*
- *Where do you feel you already have good, healthy boundaries in place?*
- *How do those boundaries make you feel?*
- *Do you find yourself saying yes, when you want to say no, or know that you should say no?*
- *Do you have trouble keeping plans? Mainly because you accept invitations that you know really you don't want to do or go to?*
- *Do you get irritable towards others, the problems they have, the expectations they have of you? Do you feel resentment towards people?*
- *Do you get really emotional at times, but you don't know or understand why?*
- *Do you feel the need to fix everyone else's problems? And please everyone around you all of the time?*
- *Do you find it difficult to ask for help and instead take on everything yourself?*

You could also find yourself experiencing some more empathic effects from your need for better boundaries:

- *Blocks in self-healing - have you ever felt like your own self-healing either isn't given priority or time, or that it simply isn't having the positive effects it used to?*
- *Wanting to help others more than care for yourself -*

do you prioritise the needs of others over your own?

- *Feeling drained energetically - would you say your energy is lower than you would like it to be? Do you feel tired a lot of the time? When you connect with your body, do you feel unbalanced and not in alignment?*

- *Absorbing other's energy and not being unable to disconnect from it - after being around other people do you feel weighed down, or start to feel physical ailments that relate to the energy of theirs that you have picked up?*

- *Taking on others fears and feelings - do you experience feelings of fear, anxiety and/or depression but know that these relate to conversations or experiences other people have shared with you?*

Finally, when you think about the answers to these questions do you feel stuck in patterns or cycles of behaviour that come up around them? How do the answers to these questions make you feel?

These questions hopefully help you get clear on a couple of things - where you need boundaries, and how important doing this work will be for you.

As I went on my own journey with boundaries, one thing became really clear to me. Where I needed to put a boundary was, more often than not, where there was a deeper wound or trauma that needed healing. These were being bought up to me by someone's behaviour or words. For me to be able to have healthy boundaries in place, there was some healing work to be done for each of them.

Healing is a really important aspect of the boundary process and work. When we take the time to do the work and heal as we put our boundaries in place, they will be strong and effective for us. It is a part of the journey that isn't necessarily reflected on much - but I feel it's actually the most important part - because we want these boundaries to improve our lives, to be healthy, and not waiver!

From going to a space where I had loads of people around me, where I thought my only struggle was finding the crowded bars and pubs they wanted to hang out in overwhelming for my senses, I started to see that actually the issue was that some people just wanted my ear, my kindness, and my energy. When I didn't have to give them? I had nothing for them.

So, I found myself in a lonely place with very few people showing up for me. At my worst, I saw other people's darker sides clearly. One person - someone who would tell people we were close friends - actually commented that they thought the operation I'd had was *"Just a procedure"*, and *"People have little prangs in cars all the time"*, so that's why they hadn't checked in with me!

Time for reflection

To heal, I had to look at many aspects, but firstly how I valued myself. I had to dig deep and learn to understand that when I showed the world that I didn't value myself enough to put me at the top of my own priority list, I attracted people that didn't consider me to be of much value either. It's that Law of Attraction thing!

For me, this pattern had shown itself to me - I didn't have the self-love or the mindset of valuing myself highly enough, so I put other's need before my own. This in turn, given my empath tendencies, attracted the wrong people to my energy, who I allowed to take advantage of me. These people didn't value me enough, much like I didn't value myself.

I hope this demonstrates a little of how identifying the pattern identifies the healing work that can be needed, and there will be more in future chapters. When this healing is worked on, it really makes boundaries easier to put into place.

In fact, when I drilled deep into why people's behaviours would trigger me, why I would feel uneasy having a boundary in a situation, and why I would give too much and not say no - self-worth was at the root of a lot of my own issues. You may find issues of self-worth, and how you value yourself, at the heart of many of your boundary issues too. Other issues that can arise are, but are not limited to:

- Fear of being our authentic self — perhaps because of being bullied or experiencing similar behaviours in our past.

- Poor sense of identify — people-pleasers (and many spiritually minded people fall into this category) tend to be so aware of how others think and feel and fear disappointing people so much that we can start to lose our true self to fit in with those around us.
- You may have experienced situations in childhood where your boundaries were often crossed, or not respected as much as they should have been.
- Past emotional traumas that we need to release and heal from.
- Witch wounds and/or past life experiences that we need to send forgiveness to.
- Fear based thoughts of not being good enough.

Having boundaries and doing this healing work can look very different for spiritually minded people. However, we also have an amazing toolkit available to us to support us through this work. I'm excited to share with you the healing practices, crystals, card spreads, and other 'woo ways I 'used to help me through my transition from someone who couldn't say no, until the universe stepped in and (really loudly) insisted that I did!

What lies beneath

Deep down, behind every behaviour, instinctive reaction, and habit that we have, is a reason why we are experiencing it. Often, it's difficult to identify what the reason is because it is said that 95% of our mind's activity is driven by the unconscious mind. Things we may not know lie in that part of our mind, things we cannot therefore and do not acknowledge in our day to day lives. We can't change the patterns of behaviour that stop us setting boundaries unless we understand why they exist.

It's this thinking plus my spiritual experiences and beliefs that drives me to share with people that the healing work to help us set boundaries goes so much deeper than we first know. So many times, I sat and wondered why the simple steps laid out to help me stand by my boundaries didn't fully work for me. I had to look at spiritual self and what lay deep down to work out what was happening.

The thoughts, beliefs and what we need to heal is different for all of us. I believe we need to look back to childhood, how previous generations in our family behaved and how we interpret that; even what happened to us in past lives. Traumas, patterns and cycles from all of these can affect how we live in the life - and how we live by and communicate healthy boundaries.

So why do we need to address all of this on our boundary journey? When I identified what I call "boundary blocks" - things that stopped us or hindered us living by our boundaries - for a whole range of situations, solutions came to mind, healing started, and things became really clear for me. By delving deeper and working on the thought patterns, memories and the beliefs that came from past experiences and had sat in my unconscious mind all this time, I moved them to my conscious awareness and could work with them. That's when the big shifts happened.

It took various different therapies and work to undercover some of the blocks within me, why they existed, and the various forms the reactions they took. For instance, my feelings that if I said no to the meeting the day of the car accident stemmed from me feeling that I would be perceived to not be capable, weak or that I wasn't able to do my job — a set of limiting beliefs that a lot of us share at points in our life. I believe, stepping back into my childhood, these fears in part came from the unresolved trauma of being bullied and called names in the playground at primary school. The kids in the playground found a weakness in me — namely my height, how I looked, and being a bit too studious - and made those things into words and action that tortured me for years on end.

My younger self took on the belief that you didn't show weakness, and that carried forward as an unconscious belief that manifested itself in many ways. From driving to a meeting that I had no place and no pressure to attend, to more simple things like not asking for help and support when I needed it, to saying I was 'ok 'when I was struggling.

I identified my people pleasing traits and the tendency to hide my true self had first showed in secondary school. During these years I 'liked 'the same footballers (I can't stand football) as other girls I shared classes with, talked about the bands they liked, and generally just went along with the trends rather than talking or bringing to the attention of others my own hobbies. I kept my interests in things like astrology a deeply guarded secret which stemmed I identified, from my witch wound (we'll delve deeper into witch wounds in a later chapter) — where standing out and being perceived as different in that lifetime had lead me in this one to hold the desire to just been unseen and fit in wherever possible.

Recently, I spoke with an old school friend for the first time in 18 years. She told me how she had spiritual experiences and beliefs as a teenager and how she didn't share them because of the fear of being seen as different or standing out in our secondary school. It struck me as so ironic and also sad that as friends we'd both struggled with living authentically, and what great friends and support to each other we could have been at school had we just have known.

As well as the things I could pull up from this life, many of the situations and areas where I had issues setting healthy boundaries and living by them, came from things in lifetimes gone by, past traumas, and things unidentified or unseen by me in my present. I came to see how looking into and working with past lives, witch wounds, inner child healing, using crystals and spiritual tools for support were really going to make a difference to my healing journey and allowed me to release my blocks.

So, what does lie beneath for you? How do you currently see each situation where you find it difficult to set boundaries? What do you believe could be your blocks? What if you looked deeper?

46

First, we need to understand our reactive response to a situation where we feel unable to live by the boundary we wish to have in place.

Take one situation where you know you have let people cross your boundary line.

If you take a situation where you know you let people cross that boundary line, what were the feelings that were present at that time? Describe those feelings in detail.

How do you feel blocked within this situation? What do you want to say and what is stopping you from communicating that? Describe the feelings, hesitations and fear that arise in this situation. These form your blocks

Can you put all of the above into a few short, concise sentences?

When <the situation> arises, I would like my boundary to be <insert>, but currently I am blocked by feelings of <insert your feelings>.

If you then take each situation that comes up in your life and repeat the same. I know that when you're finished, you're going to have some lightbulb moments. You may well see repeated blocks coming up for you.

Then I want you to move forward in your timeline. So, in a future time and space when a similar situation arises how would you like to react? How would you like to communicate your needs and boundaries in that situation? How would you like to feel when the situation arises, and you handle it with this new perspective and ways?

So that's what we're going to work to. The next few chapters will take you through the blocks that commonly come up for spiritually minded people and give you the healing that I believe will help with those blocks. You will start to see and feel transformation in how you handle the situations that you know you want to play out differently.

Future boundaries vision

So, let's revisit the visualisation in the last chapter. Close your eye. Take yourself back to that beach. See the sand beneath your feet, hear the waves lapping at the shore, and feel the sun on your face. Look down onto the golden sand, and there is the boundary line you drew. Think about the following - what drains you? What lights you up? What supports you? Do any of these clash or overlap? What situations, places and people fall on each side of that line in the sand?

Now call in your angels, your spirit guides, your guardian angel, your intuitive or higher self - whoever you work with. Welcome them on to the beach with you. Thank them for being in this space today and being with you to start this boundary setting work and supporting you through this journey. Then ask them "Where do I need to review my boundaries or have healthier boundaries?" and take note of what messages, thoughts, ideas or images that come through to you.

Grab a notebook and write it all down - and keep writing for as long as you like. Free write all the thoughts and emotions that come to you. There will be good and bad, positives and negatives. Things you want to keep in your life and are truly grateful for, and things that it's time to work on saying goodbye and moving on from.

Once you've written all of that down, how do you feel?

It's at this point I say that it's time to put down the book (or Kindle) and take some time to process and reflect on what has come up for you. This visualisation and free writing exercise can uncover some surprising truths and bring up a range of emotions. It can also lead to more questions to answer and emotions to process. It can bring an energy shift to adjust to. You may feel like you don't understand some of the problems, fears and feelings you have around boundaries - and that's okay! During this time, the important thing is not to not lose faith. You started this process for a reason, so don't lose resolve or the desire to heal and learn how boundaries can best serve you.

When you come back - and welcome back and well done for being here for everything you've worked on so far, and for all of what's to come - let's head back to that beach for a future boundaries meditation and intention setting visualisation:

––––––––––––––––––––––

Sitting comfortably, take a few deep breaths focusing your attention on your how your breath feels as you breathe in deeply, and out slowly. Take yourself back to your beach, with your line on the sand at your feet, and all the scenarios, people and places on each side as you left them previously. Now, from that beach scene, I want you take all you've learnt so far and in your head travel to a normal day in your life. It's a regular day, you live this day though with your boundaries comfortably in place, happily without stress or sadness, fear or heavy expectations weighing on you. Run through how that day looks, the scenarios that play out and how it feels for you. Check in with those feelings. Feel each of those feelings. Set the intention to heal, set the intention to live by healthy boundaries.

Now, with your journalling and the visualisation you have a really strong image and set of feelings that are your goals moving forward. At the same time, you have a list of things that no longer fit into what we are creating, that lay firmly on the other side of the line on the sand.

––––––––––––––––––––––

Cord cutting for healthy boundaries

We can and do form energetic cords to people, situations, objects and places that stay in our aura and drain us. I'm sure as a spiritually minded person you may have read about or experienced cord cutting and energy protection, and possibly even have a daily or regular ritual to clear these attachments from your aura.

These cords, to me, look like huge pipes — the sort of ones that come out of the back of air conditioning units. They attach us to everyday things throughout our lives and as they do so our energy travels down the pipes, at the same time the energy that the pipe (cord) binds us to also travels down the pipe to reach us.

So, cords give our energy out and through them we receive the energy of others too. This energy can be both positive and negative and forming these cords is completely normal. Some cords we form are great - they connect us to love, those that love us, happy situations and feelings of joy. Some cords however are formed from traumas, situations that make us feel anger or resentment, and other negative experiences or emotions. As energetic beings, living without boundaries gives these cords some of the optimum opportunities to form and attach themselves to us. Whilst this is normal, ideally, we want our energy to remain clear from these cords and attachments that can be draining us and dragging us down.

Imagine these cords as we go about our day to day lives. Hundreds of them potentially (maybe more) form each day. When it comes to our boundaries, imagine the cords that bind us to every situation where we've not enforced the boundaries that we needed. They also connect us to every person who tends to take advantage or drain us because we don't have boundaries in place. The energy of these situations then lingers with us and makes it more difficult for us to develop our new ways of being with healthy boundaries in place.

Cutting these cords doesn't cut the people we have the cord with or are involved in the situation we want to clear our energy from out of our lives. It just disconnects and clears the energy.

By cutting the cords that are currently keeping us attached to past situations and alike that block us from living by our boundaries, we can take our next step to help us move forward. Cord cutting is a simple tool to remove, dissolve and heal any unwanted energies that have become attached to you. It's a tool to help us grow and evolve, to let go of what no longer serves us, and helps us create space for new energy. A regular cord cutting practice helps to recover any energy that has been lost and to establish, or re-establish, healthy boundaries.

Before you begin, you may wish to clear your space by smudging with sage or incense and ensure that you have a quiet space and time where you will not be disturbed.

In your mind's eye, visualise all the cords that you have connecting you out into your world. Some of the cords like I mentioned are positive, filled with love. As you scan all the energetic cords you have you will instinctively, intuitively know which cords are unhealthy energetic attachments.

At this point, if you work with, or wish to work with, Archangels, you can call on Archangel Michael to help you cut and dissolve these unhealthy energetic cords to people, places, energies that stop or limit you from setting and living by healthy boundaries in your life. Visualise Archangel Michael and his sword cutting through each cord. If you prefer a more visual technique, you can visualise a pair of energetic scissors or knife cutting through each of these cords in turn. Visualise all these cords being cut and dissolving away into dust, helping free you from feelings of fear, resentment, anger, drain and overwhelm. Finally visualise yourself being surrounded by a bubble of protective light. This bubble will protect your energy as you go about your day.

You may wish to say the following affirmation aloud or to yourself: "I now cut, dissolve and release any and all energetic cords that do not serve my highest good. I release you and I release me from these attachments. I banish these energetic cords and call back any of my energy and power lost to me through these attachments. I create now the peaceful energetic boundary of love."

After cutting these cords take a few moments to sit and ground yourself.

Keeping our energy clear and protected will help our boundaries.

This cord cutting ritual isn't a one-off process. Bookmark this point and return to it however often you need to. This may be, especially while you work through the process of this book, a daily ritual. As your journey progresses, it may be less often-if you feel like you're wavering or have been through a particularly difficult time. As you tune into your own energy, you'll know how often to repeat this and what is right for you. You can then either repeat this process or add it to any daily energy clearing and protection rituals that you have and do.

The following chapters take you through various healing processes to help you further still with your journey. They will help you get to the deep roots of where I believe many of our boundary blocks come from and lie. To fully heal these blocks that make our boundaries difficult to live with in a healthy way, we need to approach the healing from a multi-dimensional nature. Both spiritually and practically. We are not just this one physical body and the thoughts and feelings we have in the present day - we are our inner child, and all the lifetimes we and our ancestors, have ever lived.

These healings can be done in any order, at any time, as often as you feel called to repeat or revisit them. You will find that they do bring things up for you that you haven't in this lifetime acknowledged or been aware of. I recommend keeping a notebook of your progress and repeating this cord cutting ritual throughout. You will explore and find out things you may now currently know or realise about yourself. Making this a constant of my spiritual practice has supported me through this journey and growth.

Part Two: Healing

Getting Comfortable with the Uncomfortable

Healing journeys are never easy, and there is a very real part of this journey where we have to get comfortable with the uncomfortable — our shadow self, the fact we cannot fix everyone, and the fact we may at times face confrontation.

With the light, comes the dark

Simply put, our shadow self is those parts of our traits and personality that we find hard to accept. Our shadow is the thoughts, feelings and emotions that we find the most painful, embarrassing even, to accept. Anger and jealously, for example. Many of us fall into the trap of trying to hide these aspects of our feelings and thoughts, and cover over them. We fear them being seen by us and others and push them into our unconscious mind. I, however, am a firm believer that with light comes darkness, and that there is a balance and understanding to be found with our shadow self.

When it comes to boundaries, our shadow-self shows through

the burdens we feel, our frustrations and anger at situations we have lost control of, and the resentment towards those that push and cross any boundary we have tried, however successfully, to put into place. Our shadow pushes forward that 'everything is fine' face that we show to the world. But when we work with our shadow, we can start to fully understand the light.

Understanding our shadow will also help us understand the people around us and how that side of them is playing out when it comes to them testing our boundaries. Our shadow self can actually be a gift when it comes to our boundaries — by showing up and giving us these emotions, it can help us identify where boundaries are needed.

Being a spiritually minded person is not all love and light. Let's be very clear about that. We are still human. We will have 'dark 'or negative thoughts. But I don't even like calling them that. I'd rather just say we have thoughts — a whole range of them, complicated as they are. Because life is complex. Choosing and living with a spiritual mindset doesn't mean that we are constantly happy and bubbly, or focused on all the amazing, positive wonders of the world. In fact, we pick up on all the heavy energies. We see and feel the hardships of the world, the pain of those around us, the suffering of sentient beings, and it's a lot. Sometimes the fact we get out of bed in a world full of stories of hardship, war, pandemics and alike amazes me!

I love what Deepak Chopra says in his book 'The Shadow Effect'; "*The flu brings misery, but that doesn't mean you are doomed to be a miserable person"*. This sums up so well the fact that we will have these periods where everything isn't just as we would want it to, but the time won't last forever.

Whilst I believe my empathic traits and ways are indeed a gift, they are also, equally at times, things that are hard to bear. I have cried during readings and healing sessions with clients because I feel their grief, their pain, their illness — and this is after spending years learning to control those feelings and protect my energy. I still even now have to control my access to the news, and take stories in piece by piece, sometimes with the words but without imagery. But I don't shy away from this anymore. Boundaries have taught me how to work with a lot that goes on — and my, albeit profusely unpopular opinion, is that as someone following this path, I cannot turn my head and attention away from the pain in the world. I watch the news, I believe I can work with it in a way to make it accessible to me, protecting my energy and mindset, and that it's vital to know what is going on in the world. I have my boundaries with the news.

So, I have embraced my shadow self. That side of me that is angry when I feel disrespected or unheard, that feels resentful of people who try to suck the energy from me, and that gets a bit judgmental at times - because it's part of me. These are emotions that have shaped me just as much as my loving side- the one that believes in the magic of the stars and the moon, in unicorns, and crystals. The same me that works to spread love in this world wherever I can and is sharing this to help you love yourself — we are all shadow and light. Go outside on the sunniest, bluest sky, beautiful of days and there, stronger than ever, will be your shadow. Real people have shadows.

Toxic Positivity

I briefly touched on toxic positivity and this tendency in the spiritual world to only focus on the light, the positives and the miraculous when it comes to self-growth. The pressure can be to focus on what manifests abundance, high vibes and being the light. What there isn't enough of, in my opinion, is balancing our shadow self, embracing how that side can help our growth, and being vulnerable, raw and real about our journeys. Without acknowledging our shadow self, our healing and growth will never be as full and authentic as it could or should be. Pretending this side of ourselves doesn't exist won't make it go away! Let's not use our spirituality to turn away and bury anything and everything uncomfortable to us. Instead, let's face it with honesty, compassion and courage.

John Welwood first used a phrase that sums this up perfectly — 'spiritual bypassing'. This is *"the use of spiritual practices and beliefs to avoid dealing with our painful feelings, unresolved wounds and developmental needs."* For me, this sums up this attitude that if we just focus on the love and light the rest doesn't exist and it will all be ok. Let's not look to our spirituality to take or hide our human side away. Let's do the work that we need to do to embrace both – and, with that work, show others how to do the same.

"It's only when we have the courage to face things exactly as they are without any self-deception or illusion, that a light will develop out of events by which the path to success may be recognised" - I Ching

---

So, when it came to my boundaries, I asked myself a couple of simple questions. Grab that notebook and have a think and journal about them too — firstly, what were the occasions where you showed up or said yes that made you feel angry, resentful, frustrated, hurt, or any other negative emotion that springs to mind? Then, what was behind each emotion and situation that came up for me? What boundaries can I see, or feel being needed to help with this in the future?

You can also refer back to the last chapter and the list of emotions and feelings that are currently blocking you from living by your boundaries. How does each of these make you feel? These questions help us look at the patterns and themes of behaviours we experience to work on them further.

For a few months, I would journal to help me understand how all this shadow side and my emotions fitted with where I was struggling with situations in my life. One of the things that regularly came up for me was that I was angry when I felt unheard or felt like the boundaries I had were crossed. I can see now that I wasn't necessarily always unheard — I had to take responsibility for the times where I had poorly communicated my needs and allowed the boundary, as weak and wavering as it was, to be moved. I felt other people had invalidated my feelings but not respecting what I wanted — maybe they simply didn't know what I wanted as I hadn't communicated it.

I decided each time to own my reaction and emotions, and to not judge myself for reacting that way. But also, to try and see both sides. Had I communicated clearly? No, well I was angry with both me and them then — but I understood why. I also had a whole list of the boundaries I needed going forward and the behaviours around them I wanted to put into place. I suggest doing something similar.

On owning the emotions: I would write each one out and then with it a healing — not positive to eradicate it — affirmation or statement for each. For example:

My emotion: I am angry at myself for not saying that I am really uncomfortable with the idea of this trip and just going along with everyone else's plans. I'm pissed off that I made a small murmur, and no one fucking heard me as loudly as I wanted them to.

Healing affirmation: I'm scared by the idea of this trip because it feels like it will be uncomfortable for me, and I don't feel it's the best thing for my physical or mental wellbeing. I am disappointed I didn't communicate that clearly. I don't judge myself for feeling or reacting this way. I know that I need to work on where my boundary is

and communicating my fears and feelings.

Try the same for each of yours. Hopefully you can see I'm not going down the 'hey it's ok, good vibes only!' approach. I'm owning that I felt an emotion, who I felt it with, and with the healing affirmation I'm acknowledging what I need to work on. This way my shadow self is empowering me to explore my emotions and where I need to do some work. It's helping me be clear about my boundaries!

Our shadow doesn't need to be the bad guy in this journey; it can be a balanced ally who helps. This mindset takes some time to get to and embrace but I know you can get there!

Meditation was also really key while I worked on getting comfortable with my feelings. It helped me to calm my mind from the racing thoughts, where I played out situations again and again in my head. Even just 10 minutes of the calming sounds of nature to help me process the feelings with compassion helped. Or a grounding walk to bring me back to centre. Again, not to dismiss, but to help with the processing.

Remember we don't want to erase our shadow self, we just want to be aware of it, understand it and balance it. Owning our feelings and why they happen, I believe, is the best, most authentic way of bringing our shadow into balance and to bring our shadow into our boundaries. This helps us see where they can be set to benefit our lives moving forward.

Away from these more spiritual practices and what I journaled, the feelings that came up were hugely helped by working with a counsellor. If you feel this will help you, I recommend reaching out to your local professional counselling services, through your doctor or similar to seek the help you need. Some parts of healing we cannot and should not do alone. If you feel looking at your shadow side - or anything in this book - has bought up traumas or things you simply don't want to address alone and need more support on, then reaching out is the bravest and best thing you can do for yourself. Remember, taking care of ourselves is now top of our priority list. Be proud of yourself for making that decision and taking that action.

And that nicely brings me to my next thing to get comfortable with.... we can't be solely responsible for fixing, helping or pleasing everyone. That includes us and why we should seek the support of professionals when we need to.

We can't fix everyone, and we're not for everyone - and actually, everyone isn't for us!

People-pleasing is a huge burden that many spiritually minded people take on, and the desire or need to fix everyone that comes to us. We need to get comfortable with the fact we are not going to please everyone all the time, and we are not going to fix everyone. Furthermore, it's simply not our responsibility.

I want to make that really clear — it is simply not our responsibility to fix those around us. We can truly only fix ourselves. We cannot carry the weight of that on our shoulders or keep trying to fix those that have to take those steps themselves. When I think about that sentiment and doing the coaching work that I do, I realise it can sound strange. There's a distinct difference that we have to establish though between fixing everyone and doing this light work how best we can. What we can do is support people in their work, but we cannot make them do the work, only offer advice and guidance, hold space and send healing. That's the boundary line I've had to draw with family, friends and clients. It took me a long time to realise that I can't fix everyone, and I had to start to draw a line where I had helped all I could. The rest of their journey was for that person to take charge of.

'It's your responsibility to take care of your energy, but remember that other people's energy is not your responsibility. You are not responsible for other people's happiness. Every individual has the power to shift their own life; you can't do it for them." - Gabby Bernstein

I'm not saying we shouldn't care about other people, want them to be happy, want to help them, or try to support them. However, what's vital is that we don't care about others to the point where we minimise or suppress our own needs, feelings and care. We are just as important as everyone else and acting like we're not only makes our boundaries either non-existent or exceptionally difficult to live by.

During the following chapters we will address many of these aspects, and the healing within the pages, the journalling and rituals will help with each. First though, we need to get comfortable with not pleasing everyone, release the need for other people's approval, and love ourselves enough to do this work. We have to accept that we can't control how others think of us. Ultimately, how they act is their choice and says more about them than it ever does us. Not everyone is going to like us — and actually that's ok.

Imagine if everyone we met liked us and that we gelled with everyone who came by our path. Wouldn't that be exhausting? We would never have the time to facilitate all those relationships. We wouldn't appreciate the levels of friendships and family relationships we do have, because we wouldn't see the contrast with other people we'd met or experienced that bond with. So, it's ok — actually it's good — that we aren't for everyone. Because everyone isn't and shouldn't be for us!

Guilt is another common, overwhelming emotion that inhibits our boundary work. It's often a way we mask other feelings, a sign of low self-esteem (which we will work on in the chapter "*Am I Enough?*") and limiting beliefs. With our feelings of guilt around how our boundaries make someone feel, we must first acknowledge that we've done nothing wrong by having boundaries, as well as owning our boundaries as our choice to ensure that we are looking after ourselves. Then we can show love and compassion to ourselves.

During our time together in these pages I want you to remember to love yourself and show yourself love as often as you need. This might be daily, and get less as this work gets easier, and the love you show yourself gets stronger. But as we start, I want you to try and create this bliss moments regularly in your schedule where you recognise that you love yourself and you put you first. This could be by:

- *taking time for a soak in a salt bath*
- *writing a gratitude list for at least 10 things you love about yourself*
- *putting some music on that makes you feel happy and moving your body to it*
- *buy yourself some flowers*
- *take a walk-in nature to ground and connect with all the beauty around you*
- *looking at yourself in the mirror and reciting an affirmation, such as 'I am beautiful inside and out', or 'I am worthy of putting my needs first '*
- *ensure you are speaking kindly to yourself each and every day.*

During this process, I found that allowing myself to sit with the discomfort that came up if I felt rejected or judged, or that I'd let someone down was important to take the time to do. Taking a deep breath and a stepping back got me through some awkward moments where I would have gone back to people-pleasing ways. Allowing myself to sit with the feeling that came up, write it all out, and having a cry or a shout or whatever I needed to do to process felt really good.

So, when one person ghosted me (literally ghosted me) for whatever thoughts and feelings they had about me and my life, I did exactly that. I sought the opinion of two friends that I love and respect the views of, and I journaled how I felt. Every feeling that rose up was acknowledged— from the why, what the heck, what did I do, through the anger, and hurt and complete disillusion of what I thought this friend was to me. I cried and asked for hugs when I needed. I gave myself permission, time and space to do all of this. At the end I wrote out to myself ' *...she chose to do this; I am not a bad person for this choice. I accept this is her choice, but I don't let this reflect on me being who I am '.* After a few days, one morning I got up and took a bath with Epsom salts and rose quartz crystals. During that bath I thought about all the people that I have in my life who love me, and how grateful I am for those people and what we share. I got out, dried off, put some music on and danced around my house to shift my energy.

Now this might not sound like a huge thing, but before this I would have tried to find out more and sent a random *'how are you?* 'message to try and see if they'd answer (without, of course, asking directly what was going on because I struggled with confrontation). I would have dwelled on the situation, been afraid to go to venues where we used to meet in case they were there, and ran conversations and events through in my head one thousand times (and then a few more). So actually, the above was a huge transformation for me. Getting comfortable with not being for everyone and not being able to control their behaviours was freeing. It still hurt, but it doesn't have that hold on me that it would have before. I can process and move forward.

The more you go through this book and work through things, the more uncomfortable feelings from our shadow self and dealing with those around us will arise. But just remember, both serve us in their different ways, and both can help us get to where our goal is.

We can't fix everyone, and we're not for everyone. And that's just fine with me!

Can confrontation be comfortable?

The type of fear that comes with the idea of confrontation is hard to explain. Situations and conversations that may lead to confrontations can be especially uncomfortable for spiritually minded people. We find these situations overwhelming and unpleasant. The energy of these situations is particularly heavy and draining for us, and sometimes we find confrontation simply terrifying.

One thing to get comfortable with on our boundary journey is the idea that confrontation can be a positive experience in the long-term. If we can learn to handle confrontation in a healthy way and an approach that we are comfortable and at easy with, this only makes setting and communicating our boundaries easier for us.

Confrontation can be handled with grace and, whilst it goes against our people pleasing ways, can help us reach healthy conclusions to situations with people. It can help us stand by our boundaries and can support our growth. Standing up for ourselves is allowed, and we can create a safe space for this.

So, what situation comes to mind when you think about confrontation? Grab your journal and write about all the feelings this situation and possible confrontation bring up for you.

Then think about what your ideal outcome in this situation would be. Without confrontation how would the conversation or scene play out?

Then ask yourself the following questions:

- *What do you stand to lose if you confront this person/people?*
- *What do you stand to lose if you don't?*

- *What are the risks?*
- *Would you go ahead with the confrontation even though your fears might be realised? Why or why not?*
- *If your fears were realised, how would you live with the result?*

Next, we plan what we want to say - what does it look at to stay aimed at our idea outcome and clearly communicate our side of this situation. With a plan in place these sorts of conversations can be made much easier.

Then take some time to meditate and during that meditation send loving, compassionate thoughts to the situation. Breathe in confidence and breath out your fears.

When the time comes take all your plan and all of the feelings from the meditation and these will both help and support you.

With any confrontation, remember that you have the right to be heard, the right to stand up for yourself, and to listen. We all know there are two sides to every situation. Remember that the person/people you're talking to will have a reaction, and that may be a very emotional response. Take calming deep breaths and know that you can always pause, step away and come back to this later. Ultimately, remember that you've come into this situation with a healthier situation moving forward as your goal.

The healing that comes from getting comfortable with what is uncomfortable for us holds us in a great space as we move towards healthy boundaries.

Am I Enough?

A lot of boundary issues stem from a lack of self-worth. When we don't value ourselves and experience a lack in this area, we can feel like boundaries are impossible to live by — and if we do try to, we generally let people cross them a lot of the time.

About 18 years ago, my self-esteem and self-worth were at their worst. As it is with many people, the problems and thoughts had really kicked in at the start of my teens. During this time, a lot of my behaviour and actions (I now see) came from a place of low self-worth and no boundaries. From drinking until I didn't remember whole days and nights and what had happened, to accepting some pretty awful behaviour from other people.

One night I remember being at a gig my boyfriend (although I now call him husband) was playing. A guy was there who was in the circle of people that we seemed to be spending more and more time with socially. Everyone seemed to love this guy. He was the life and soul of the party, always organising night's out and getting people together.

After the gig finished, a couple of girls were talking to the band members. It was flirty, you could tell, and of course that did nothing for the young girl I was who didn't love herself much at all at this time. So, this guy from the friendship circle is talking quite loudly. I'm stood only one person away, so well within ear shot, and I hear him say, *"Well, he'd do better taking her home than the minger he's with".* The 'he' being my boyfriend, the 'minger' being me.

That wasn't the only occasion I'd hear him say it. He'd rhyme minger with my maiden name - alliteration and rhyme being such a great joke. I would feel horrendous anytime a social occasion was bought up, but I would go, wondering why he was so popular and loved by everyone it seemed. Did no one else see through him? Was I the only one? Or did they all simply agree with what he was saying about me? I would hate these thoughts more and more, I would hate how I looked more, and I was quickly becoming more and more insecure.

I thought at the time that I had to fit in, so I had to put up with this behaviour and me being the only one on the inside feeling so, so different. And without a boundary to be seen I never said a word. Until I just typed that.

Low self-worth and a lack of boundaries is so damaging to us. It takes away the one love we should all have — the love of ourselves and seeing the amazing, special and unique individuals we all are. No matter what we look like, believe in or how we live our lives. It makes us keep ourselves small for the sake of other people. It makes us live in fear or never being good enough, and potentially never shining as bright as we should.

The question of 'am I enough?', the fears and doubts that

linger around how we feel about ourselves, and our limiting beliefs form another huge block to living by our boundaries. If we feel like we may not be all we want to be to everyone and that we don't fit or fulfil other people's expectations, we can push ourselves to try and fill the gap that we perceive to exist. We look to fill that gap with the acceptance of others, and this dependance on their validation, brings in a cycle of people-pleasing behaviours.

How does this manifest with boundaries? So, for me, it drove the desire to fit in and to help people all of the time.

Am I enough?
No, well I should try to be more.

Am I enough?
No, well I have to help more then.

Am I enough?
No, then I need to try and fit in more.

In my desire to fit in with people, whether they were right for me or not, I lost my true self and kept her hidden deep down. It also drove a lot of thoughts of self-comparison that led me to say yes to things I wasn't happy with or comfortable with. If people around me were saying yes, why wasn't I? If they were doing this, why wasn't I? I would compare myself to other people too, and this would make me feel like I was failing and not good enough again in so many ways.

Away from my spiritual self, the fears around not being enough led to out-of-control thoughts and deep anxieties. Was I enough at work? No, push more then, take on more, whether I had the time and knowledge or not.

These spiralling thoughts bought about a lot of drain, overwhelm and negative energy - as you can imagine — and all of which could have been stopped if I'd just been true to myself and my boundaries.

The expectations of others also holds us in a place of fear that we are not enough. Sometimes these expectations are down to how people have reacted in the past. Sometimes I believe that we also project what we feel people's expectations will be before we have even spoken to them.

People pleasing is a common issue we face, and we need to start healing the fear that causes this behaviour and subsequently drains us because we always put other people before ourselves. This fear of being criticised by others, that we won't be liked, or we'll be rejected, all manifest with people pleasing behaviour. It can be an unconscious impulse, especially with spiritually minded people. For many of us it goes hand in hand with finding conflict difficult, our need to fit in, the guilt that saying no brings us, and honestly, a lack of self-love.

The fear of what will happen when we say no and start putting ourselves first can also be a difficult block to overcome. But how much of that fear is projected and how much is real?

What do I mean?

Have you had the conversation where you said no and were rejected? You probably have in the past - and from that we have a very real, very human and understandable tendency to project that one scenario onto future conversations and situations. We run through what will happen in our heads, through the whole conversation, ending at the point where we're rejected again. And I'd bet - from personal experience - that we do that, and it isn't always the case.

Have you watched the American drama '*This Is Us*'? Two of the characters, Randall and Beth, are shown playing a game - the Worst Thing That Could Happen game. They run through a situation and between them, going back and forth, take it to the extreme worst case scenario end. This isn't just a game in a television show, it's actually based on an exercise in Dialectical Behaviour Therapy. It's also a super relatable moment in the show because let's be really honest here, we all do it at times!

I believe we sometimes do this when it comes to how we interact with people. We play out how saying no will go in our heads before we've even had the conversation. We decide on the other person's behalf that saying no will be taken very badly, and that they will judge us, reject us, and ultimately never speak to us again.

But - what if we just try and say no? Or what if we try and

tell them how we truly feel in our heart? How will they actually react?

I know personally it's gone both ways. But very rarely has the "my worst-case game 'scenario played out. For instance, when a friend who I thought would be very anti my spiritual work was actually really interested and asked me questions when they found out. I didn't honestly at first know how to react - because I'd done this chat already in my head - but it was great. They were really, truly interested. Although they don't share my beliefs, they wanted to know how and why I followed this path and what it had bought to my life. It was a great discussion and it proved to me that my brain didn't always win that game!

This game we play in our heads is us and our ego communicating — that voice in our heads that tries to protect us. Our ego is that part of our mind that either consciously or subconsciously brings anxieties, worries and fears into our lives. That's it's purpose — it's how it keeps us protected.

Now, you would think the ego would love our boundaries because our boundaries in many ways protect us. But our ego fights against our boundaries because it hasn't set them. You see, our boundaries do not come from our ego. Our ego wants to control, comes from a space of judgement, separation and overreaction. Our boundaries come from a place of love and our authentic self. Whilst they can protect us, it is not the sole purpose of our boundaries. Our boundaries empower us, and our ego is uncomfortable with that.

So how can we overcome all of this? Both with an ego set on protection, and fears that play out and make us people-pleasers?

First, we need to identify what's happening. So, it's time to grab your journal!

- *When are you being true to yourself around people?*
- *When are you saying, doing or behaving in a way because you think that's what people expect and want you to do?*
- *How do these times make you feel?*
- *Can you identify any of these feelings as your ego trying to protect you?*
- *Take one event or scenario as an example - how would you behave, what would you say or do if you acted if you were being 100% authentic and true to yourself?*

To then have the confidence to fully live by our boundaries we need to embrace loving and accepting ourselves, believing that we are enough - just the way we are.

Reflect on your answer to the final question - and resolve that next time you're going to behave, say and do, being 100% authentic and true to yourself.

I now firmly see and believe we are each enough. Perfectly imperfect as we are- we are enough. Remember perfection doesn't exist, thank goodness! How boring would that truly be? We are all unique with different gifts, traits, values and we all are enough. Being enough isn't about perfection - It's about accepting who we are, flaws and all. It's about embracing that we are human and giving ourselves the safe space we need to grow. And by working on ourselves, just like we are with this book, we are doing that.

It took me a while to realise I was enough as I am. Actually, now at times I would credit myself with being more than enough. I show up and I try, and I love with an open heart. So, for me, I am enough.

We are enough, we always have been, and we always will be. You are enough. We just need to accept and welcome that mindset:

- *Meditate daily reciting the mantra "I am enough '*
- *Remember that what you see on social media and how others show their lives to be, is generally them putting their best out to the world — it's rarely the full truth of their life and current situation. It's just what they choose to show the world.*

- *Remind yourself daily of at least 3 things you love about yourself.*
- *Regularly take time to do something that makes you happy - without worrying about other people - just because it will bring you joy. It doesn't have to be something big (although it can be if you wish), but just take some day to indulge in something that lights you up. Schedule it in your diary if that will help you stick to it!*

Finally, when it comes to self-love and acceptance, look at yourself through the eyes of others, the way your spirit guides, angels, or whoever spiritually you feel most called to work with see you. Your guides stand with you, encouraging you to see yourself how they do. Each and every day, take some time to love yourself, speak to yourself kindly, and remember how your guides see you. Keep aligned with love and the rest will flow.

"Accept that you are enough. You don't need to be anything that you are not." - Wayne Dyer

Our Inner Child

I mentioned previously how the events of our childhood can form the basis of some of the problems we have living by our boundaries. I think, as a population, we now understand more how that crucial period during our younger years informs our behaviour as adults. If at any time during your childhood you had your boundaries crossed, ignored, didn't feel safe or seen or heard, then issues may surface when having healthy boundaries in place as adults.

"Having your emotions consistently invalidated as a child and one day waking up as an adult expected to validate your own emotions in order to set boundaries and trust your feelings over everyone else is an extremely wild experience. Be gentle with yourself. You're learning." – Gaia

Now you may not have been spiritual as a child, or you may have known your gifts but not understood them. You may even have been that kid that just knew you were different and didn't know why! Personally, my childhood was filled with what I now understand to be my gifts - I would talk to animals, I knew that stars were magical, I had these presences around me that gave me advice and guidance, and had a way of knowing when the energy of somewhere or someone wasn't the energy I wanted around me. I didn't like the popular kids at school. I now know that to be part of my witch wound showing through. I didn't trust the groups like that or the individuals within them. So, whether you feel like that same scared kid, or a different person to when you were a child, inner child healing can still benefit your boundaries.

I didn't know where to start with inner child healing. To think back bought up a lot. The loss of my beloved Nanny stood out — and instilled a lifelong fear of death and loss that goes beyond what I'm covering in this book, and still have healing work to do on. I recalled being bullied in primary school for not being one of the 'cool kids' and a bit too studious. I remembered being judged in secondary school for how I looked and what I wore. For having a diary of mine read and, like so many teenagers, feeling lost and needing to understand and explore who I was becoming. Most of all, I thought back to a longing and constant desire to fit in — whatever that may take, and to keep people happy so they liked me and with the hope that the loneliness I'd felt so often wouldn't return.

All of this led to some bad, almost dangerous, situations that played out in my late teenage years and into my early twenties, which, as I started this journey, I still carried the guilt and shame for deep down. I had never held myself, or my body in particularly, with the value we should all hold ourselves to.

It also meant I never showed weakness to others or asked for help when I needed it… until it was almost too late. I was taught and told that you stood up to the bullies. That first and foremost you didn't show them that they were getting to you. A teacher told my parents once that one day the mouse (me) turned and roared at the bullies like a lion. I'd shouted back at the bullies. I don't remember the moment and I've tried many times to recall it. I think my brain has shut it out because it knows that that was an act and not the real me.

Inner child healing

That mindset of never showing weakness was instilled at that point and led to me never admitting any sort of vulnerability, and never being able to say no when I needed to protect my body, health and mindset. Your experiences will show up differently for you too, and it's important to identify why you feel triggered or scared, as well as being aware of anytime you feel like the child within you needs holding, witnessing and understanding. So, let's focus on boundaries and where our inner child needs healing to help you with this.

Maybe you were bullied, struggled to find where you fitted in, didn't feel seen or safe, had your own boundaries ignored and overstepped — all of these events, and similar experiences, will have had an effect. It's completely normal and common as adults that when circumstances cause similar feelings to come up that we feel triggered and like we regress back to that phase of our lives.

While we can't change the past, inner child healing works with the part of our psyche that is our childhood; the memories, feelings and events from those years of our lives.

No matter what you experienced in childhood, this healing can work with you. I find it hard to find anyone who didn't experience something during their childhood that affects them now — whether that be big traumas, abuse, neglect, the loss of family members or friends, being bulled, having issues with sexuality, or struggles finding yourself and the path that's for you in this life. This healing work brings about an understanding and sends love to your inner child. It isn't about forgetting the experiences you had but assuring the child who still remains within us that everything will be ok and that they are safe now.

Childhood and our teenage years can be difficult times when communicating our boundaries is especially difficult as many of us are still in a period of searching and finding ourselves. Add in the hormones, pressures and expectations of school and exams, and all of those other teenage joys and it's a turbulent time for many.

One of the most powerful exercises I've been through to uncover the blocks to living by my boundaries explored what was at the core of my issues. It looked at what was the very first occasion my boundaries have been crossed and essentially when I first felt like my power and ability to ask anyone to respect those boundaries had been taken away. Let's do it together now:

_____

So, grab that journal and ask yourself the following, free write whatever comes through and rises up within you:

- *What's the first time you remember your boundaries feeling / being crossed as a child?*
- *Visualise the scene in your head. Describe the situation - where are you? Who is involved? What age are you? What do you see, hear, taste and feel? Be as specific as you can be to help you build the fullest picture possible.*
- *What feelings come up for you at this time? What is the main emotion you are feeling at this time?*
- *If you have more than one memory come up, that's fine. Visualise and journal each one separately.*

Once you got all of that written down let's go into a visual meditation exercise. If you have had more than one memory come back to you, start with the one where you are youngest. That first memory, as small as you are, is where the first boundary block was installed. So, we start with healing our earliest memory first. As you begin to settle for the next stage in this ritual feel free to burn some sage, light a candle, get comfortable sitting or lying down and place your journal to one side.

Now closing down your eyes, I want you to build up a picture in your mind's eye of that memory, the one in the scene you just wrote about.

- *Visualise everything you wrote down, the place you're in, who is with you, anything you see, smell, hear or feel.*

- *Now I want you to see yourself in that scene, at the age you were then. See what you look like, what you're wearing, where you are in that moment.*
- *Then I want you to just take that all in for a moment. Clearly see it in your mind's eye. The more details that you notice and spring up it now feels almost 3D and like the present day you is an observer on this image.*
- *Now visualise adult you, you of the present moment, stepping into that scene and walking over to your child self. Sit down with them and say hi and introduce yourself. Spend a few moments just connecting with them and their energy. Reassure them that you are here to help them.*
- *Now for the next few minutes I want you to have a conversation with your child self. Ask them how they are feeling? What do they perceive is happening in this scene? What's their side of this story? How does having their boundary crossed make them feel?*
- *Ask your child self what they need to help them right now. Visualise yourself providing the hug, love, reassurance, whatever it is they need most right now.*
- *Promise your child self that they are seen, heard, loved and safe and that you are here to help them and look after them. Make a promise that you will keep working with them to help both of you moving forwards.*
- *As you say goodbye to your child self, visualise yourself stepping out of the scene and back into your current surroundings, bring yourself slowly back to*

the current time and the space you're sat in.

- *Journal everything that came up for you during this experience.*

Following this, you can go into a meditation and connect with your child-self energy at any time. Remember the promise you've made them and connect back often. Whether it's buying a colouring book, listening to music, sending them a hug, doing an activity that brings your child self, or simply wearing a favourite colour. Honouring them and working with them will help this healing continue- your connection will remain strong, and your inner child will feel safe and loved as you continue this boundary work. I keep a teddy that reminds me of my childhood close when doing any of this work. As soon as I feel my inner child needing that extra care and empathy, or something triggers me and relates back to childhood, I'll give the bear a hug. For me, it's a tangible symbol of that connection and helps me continue this healing journey.

Witch Wounds, Past Lives and Soul Contracts

Hiding our authentic self and not allowing ourselves to be heard and seen for who we truly are is a common problem, and it makes having healthy boundaries difficult.

I mentioned before my life in Narnia. When I was so far into living in my spiritual closet, with the misunderstood witch being me, one of my cats played Aslan and the other was my Mr. Tumnus! Seriously though, I was stuck in this closet between the magical life I wanted to live, and my regular life. While Narnia and my wardrobe are metaphors, they provide a scarily accurate picture for how life felt. No wonder it was one of my favourite books as a child!

I know I'm not alone when it comes to fear at showing our authentic selves to those around us. I know many spiritually minded people struggle with this aspect of their journey. Seeing those around us be so open with their beliefs can make you feel even more of a failure, or unworthy of this path. It was, and probably quite honestly remains, the hardest part of my journey. To lift the lid on this aspect of myself and my life that was a secret to so many.

As an empath, for years I found sitting in busy bars and clubs really difficult. The overwhelm felt with the loud music, crowds of people, the darkness, and flashing lights. My senses couldn't cope. I would get panic attacks, and drink more than I should to try and relax. The alcohol made my body ill and feel awful. In my late teens and early 20s, inauthentic me who was desperate to feel "normal" would embark on Friday and Saturday nights of this environment week after week, only because it was the "done thing".

To the world, I had very few boundaries and they were, at best, blurry. Blurry boundaries, which we often let people cross, can erode our sense of identity, making it difficult for us (and people around us, if they're paying close attention) to really know who we are and what we stand for. I did things that I look back on with shock at times (and took some healing work to understand and be understanding of). Most of my behaviour came from the fear of the reactions people would have if I said no- what they would say, what they would think of me, and how I would be judged.

No, I don't want to go clubbing.

No, I don't like those sorts of nights out.

No, I don't want drink alcohol tonight…

…how would they react to me? I feared feeling lonely and judged.

I don't know what people would have thought or said had I actually been honest about any of that. I had, however, written their reactions in my head. I'd assumed they would react badly to me, would no longer have any interest in hanging out with me, and would talk about me and my "weird" or "unfriendly" behaviour to others. Because in my head that was their reaction, I never tested it in the real world.

In later years, this fear reared its head again as I started on the second, and much deeper, phase of my spiritual journey. My fear of what those closest to me who didn't share or fully understand my beliefs would think meant I put myself deep into the spiritual closet. At this time, I had a good life, a close circle of friends, my husband, family and a corporate career that was going well.

I feared the judgement that might come, and I wondered how people would take this new person that was coming forward. Would my friends remain the same? Would people 'get 'me? What about those people who I knew for certain saw spirituality, crystals, energy healing and alike as some farfetched, fantastical thinking? How would new me fit in old me's life and circles?

Well, the truth is, there was no new me and old me. There was me - the rest was the show and front woman hiding the girl who just wanted to fit in. I'm sure many of you are the same, because this is our soul, and it's deep within us until we allow our gifts, empathic ways and energies to flood out.

As I wrote in Chapter Two, my experience on the weekend with Kyle Gray opened the door to that closet. There was a definite crack of light shining though. I took baby steps. It's taken years and I've done it a way I'm comfortable with. This book will blast the last of that closet door off the hinges!

Our fear of people's reactions is one of the many reasons we don't enforce our boundaries. We assume and presume that people will take our "no" badly, which they might. But the way I look at that now is that their response says more about them than me. We fear any confrontation that our responses and actions may lead to. Honestly, when I now say no and explain my no, I rarely get a bad response. Even recently I said no to a hen night invite. I explained I can't really do busy bars and nightclubs. for I find them overwhelming and lead me to panic attacks. I'd rather the ladies enjoyed themselves than had to worry about me. The response was lovely - we get it, we'll miss you, let's catch up soon.

Fear of not fitting in, being judged, fear to live as our authentic self, fear of being open with our spiritual beliefs- these things all may stem from a witch wound.

The witch wound and past life traumas

The witch wound is a deep trauma, experienced in lifetimes gone and possibly, whilst in different ways and different lifetimes, we may have experienced similar feelings and events many times in our past lives. When we experience a trauma a number of times, each occurrence buries itself deeper into our DNA.

Simply put, our witch wound - or a past life trauma - is the concept that in one or more past lives we, or someone in our lineage, were punished in some way for our beliefs and the lifestyle that we lived.

Being a "witch" actually meant that you were a wise woman

within your community, someone who people would go to for advice, for healing, or for offerings of some sort. These wise women were midwives, they worked with herbs, held space for people, and worked with the cycles of the moon. Some were considered witches for simply having red hair or a cat.

Between 1400 and 1762, women like those I've just described were branded witches. Many were hunted, tortured, and it is estimated that 35,000 to 50,000 people were sadly killed for their beliefs and way of life, or simply the suspicion and fear of what their way of life may be or mean.

If you're a man reading this book, please don't feel like this chapter doesn't hold anything for you. Firstly, the gender type we identify with in this lifetime is not necessarily the same throughout our past lives. Secondly, I've heard one statistic that says that as much as 20% of those people who were killed were male. Men who bravely chose to stand up for the women being accused or who tried to protect them were also persecuted in this way. Many men simply saw what was happening, and those images and the knowing of what happened caused a witch wound to exist within them.

We carry this wound deep within us, whether we experienced it directly or it has been passed to us through our lineage. It makes us feel not safe to fully embrace our spiritual power, to not live authentically as we are. It makes us not want to speak in public, to not use our voice, to not trust other women, and to not speak up for ourselves. As an effect of our witch wound, we may hide ourselves away, diminish ourselves, close off our gifts and ignore our intuition.

As generations passed, we found ourselves, unknowingly, living by a pact to keep ourselves safe. We resolved to not shine, to not stand out, to hold our gifts buried within and to not speak out. This pact, and all of the associated fears, has been passed down for generations.

Our witch wound and boundaries

But how does this witch wound come into our lives when we look at it from the perspective of boundaries?

Having and living with healthy boundaries in place means we speak up for ourselves, allowing people to see the true and most authentic version of ourselves, without hiding behind anyone or anything or fearing the reactions of those around us.

When it comes to our boundaries, this is how a witch wound can show up through:

- Fear of being labeled as "different" or "other" or "bad"
- Fear of living authentically, with freedom of your personal beliefs
- Fear of speaking out and/or being seen
- Not sharing your feelings and/or opinions for fear of confrontation

- Isolation from others and their support
- A mistrust of other women or men who are not in your "inner circle"

This is, of course, not an exhaustive list, but as you can see, there are plenty of ways in which this wound shows itself to us.

During a past life reading my witch wound came to light. *A lifetime lived in a region of Germany where I advised people on what to do for their best future, gave them herbs from a forest nearby to heal themselves, and helped women give birth and heal afterwards with remedies and tinctures.*

But, as with any witch wound, the townspeople - especially the males - called me a witch and I was driven out of town, eventually hunted and killed for my beliefs.

Past lives and boundaries

If you don't identify with a lifetime where you were believed to be a witch, you can still experience a witch wound or similar trauma that's carried forward. Other past lives of mine had incidents and themes not dissimilar from that of my witch lifetime, and therefore instilled a similar wound.

In Ancient Egypt, I saw myself in a street market setting, then being grabbed from that street and jailed for helping street children by passing foods and remedies for their health to them. I was told of a lifetime where I was betrayed by a woman close to me because she didn't like the advice I was giving the community. Whilst not as clear as the other lifetimes, I was obviously judged for doing what spiritually I am consistently, lifetime after lifetime called to do - help people.

It all sounded and felt very traumatic, as you can imagine. I was shocked at what had come up in the reading. To feel that fear in this day and know that this trauma had been carried through was, however, enlightening. It took a while to process how I felt and bring all the pieces together. Now, in case you're worried about getting a past life regression, please don't be. Find someone recommended to you or that you trust and see it as opportunity to help things you just can't put a finger on make sense. See it as the opportunity to open up and discover so much more about yourself and your gifts. Having that spiritual connection to so many lifetimes helped me connect and have confidence with my intuitive gifts too. And it won't all be trauma filled! The reader also revealed to me two lifetimes where me and my husband were together - one particularly lovely lifetime in France in the late 1700s, perhaps the universe's gift to me was this lifetime filled with love and dancing in royal courts! Perhaps that lifetime was presented to me to help heal and show my soul a lighter side of life following my witch hunt and other traumas.

Revealing my past - and all those lifetimes - was amazing, enlightening and overwhelming all in one. I started to piece together fears and behaviours in this lifetime that I believe were all linked to this witch wound and the resulting feelings made it difficult for me to stick by boundaries in this life.

How could I set boundaries - even fully understand them and the work needed - if I couldn't fully speak up for myself, if fear of people's rejections and judgements haunted me and triggered deep trauma, if I couldn't voice my opinions for fear of confrontation, and ultimately if my soul remembered that standing up for how I wanted to live had only caused me to be hunted, killed and betrayed before?

But how to heal a witch wound or a past life trauma? Now, whether you have experienced a past life reading or not, whether you have seen and recognised a witch wound or other trauma previously, or this is your first idea or acknowledgement of this lying deep within you, you can still work with this energy and heal.

First though, I feel that it's important that we honour this witch wound. It's not a wound to dismiss or take lightly. As a collective, women were persecuted. As gifted beings, they were judged, hunted and punished. First of all, I think it's important that as part of that collective we honour them, and we recognise and honour our part in this moment of history and time. How you honour this I will leave up to you - you will know how you feel best able to and are called to do this. My suggestions are to spend some time reading the stories that are in history books and archives and delve into some of the experiences and what happened. Light a candle and spend some time acknowledging the effect this wound has had on your life. Honour the witch in you now and feel pride in the gifts and knowledge you have. Offer those that lived through that time our thanks and gratitude for all they gave for us. If you want to discover more about the witch inside of you, I recommend '*Witch - Unleashed, Untamed, Unapologetic*' by Lisa Lister as a great book to delve into.

Now I want you to draw your attention inwards. How does this witch wound affect you? Do you resonate with any of the following:

- *Acting differently around people to fit in because of a fear of being seen as "different" or "other" or "bad"*
- *Fear of sharing your spiritual or personal beliefs with others because of what they might say or think*
- *Fear of public speaking, or speaking up for yourself*
- *Fear of or unable to cope with situations that may lead to confrontation*
- *Imposter syndrome around your intuitive abilities and gifts*
- *Keeping problems to yourself and feeling unable to ask for help or support*
- *Finding it difficult to trust people, keeping your close circle small*

How do you feel your wound plays out in your day to day? Obviously pay special attention to where you feel it has affected your ability to set and live by your boundaries.

Specific events, circumstances, people may all come up for you. I'm big on journalling (you might have noticed) so grab a pen and get it all down on paper. Take some time in contemplation to think about each point and whether you recognise that in your behaviour:

- *When it comes to your life and your boundaries, where are you not speaking your truth?*
- *When and where do you feel like you cannot speak up?*
- *Is there something you'd like to do or say, but the fears of how other people will react stop you?*
- *Do you hide your beliefs and gifts? Or do you over share them and let people take too much and drain you?*
- *With the healing of your witch wound, what could, or would you do?*

Spend some time with all that comes up.

Take some deep breaths, with one hand on your sacral chakra and one hand on your heart chakra. Direct your breath to both of these areas. Just breathe. Where are your feelings, thoughts about your witch wound and fears coming up for you? Pay attention to any areas of your body where you are feeling them. Send your breath and loving energy to these areas.

Repeat the mantra: "I am safe. It is safe for me to be in my body".

Set the intention to reclaim any power lost through your witch wound: "I reclaim my power and my magic, my wisdom and my ability to be me in my truth, and to use my voice."

Now I want you to move your body, put on your favourite tune, the music that makes you feel your best and most magical self. I want you to dance, and move, and give yourself a hug. Embrace yourself and all the wonder that you are.

You've got this!

You can repeat this healing as many times as you need.

Soul Contracts and Spiritual Agreements

As my healing journey progressed, I came to understand the influences energy from before this lifetime had on my current way and being, and the idea of soul contracts intrigued me.

Soul contracts can be defined as an agreement your soul took on at the start of all your lifetimes, before you were born, and this contract comes into play during every life you live here on Earth. These contracts are not just about the relationships we have each lifetime, they involve the life events, circumstances and situations that we live through. Spiritual agreements can be seen in a similar way. These agreements are in place to teach us the lessons we need to learn throughout a lifetime.

In these soul contracts, we determine how we reach our purpose in this lifetime and form many of the family and friendships that we experience; these are the people bought into our lives to help us reach that purpose. So, how does this show itself in our ability to live by and set boundaries?

Soul contracts can be both what we would perceive as good and bad. Connections that bring love and pain, darkness and light — it all drives us forward. Remember what I've said before: we're here to have a human experience- both the positive and negatives- and we have to experience both. The lows help us realise, appreciate and have gratitude for the highs. Soul contracts and their effects can help us achieve our unique purpose in life.

Sooner or later, soul contacts or agreements will show up in our lives and show us where we need to heal. One of the most healing things your contracts do is help you become a better person. You become conscious of your behaviours and, if you do the healing work, you raise your vibration, changing your energy from fear to love. As you heal, you heal those around you - your energy always influences those around you.

Could bad boundaries, or needing to learn the lessons of boundaries, be part of a soul contract or agreement made before you were born? We've established that they can be the effect of a trauma from past lives, so could they be part of your bigger drive to achieve your soul purpose? Could learning the lessons of not having healthy boundaries be something you are destined to do through this contract? Could the people pushing and crossing our boundaries have been part of this contract to help us learn these lessons?

I believe this to be true. The repeated patterns I mentioned, where my boundaries were crossed or just simply not in place lifetime after lifetime, are a sign that this was also in part due to a soul contract, or a number of soul contracts and agreements, being in place. The fact that it was a repeated trauma I could see time and time again, showed that my learning wasn't complete, so it kept coming up as an issue.

In this lifetime I believe that the contracts I have that are around boundaries are to be fulfilled; they are driving me and my purpose. I am not only learning the lessons, but also sharing them to heal and to finally fulfil this contract to move on.

So, when we're learning these lessons, repeating the patterns, asking ourselves why we wavered, or letting someone cross our boundaries, don't see it as a failure. That was one of the big lightbulb moments for me. It's not a failure as we go through this journey. It's not a failure at any point in our futures. It's a lesson to be learnt that will drive us forward and serve a purpose perhaps larger than we can understand at this point.

We are of course also people with free will. So, should we feel a soul contract is in place, and actually we don't want it anymore- that is for us to choose. Just because we signed up to these contracts at birth, doesn't mean that we can't change our minds and the direction we consciously decide to take this lifetime. We also have the choice to learn the lessons - which I believe is the choice, consciously or unconsciously that you have been guided to make and would have, I'm sure, led to you to this book.

If you choose to, you can cancel this contract. Give yourself some time in a quiet place. Cleanse the space with sage and light a candle. Take a few deep breaths and a moment in meditation to centre yourself. Then recite the following:

"I cancel, clear, delete and release old conditionings, karmic contracts, soul contracts, vows, repetitive negative patterns, repetitive negative energy, generational curses, and ancestral karma. Those energies end now as they are no longer aligned with who I came here to be in this present time. May all those effected by these energetic contracts to me be released so our should are free to evolve and move on."

By learning the lessons and doing the healing work, we are honouring this contract. We are fulfilling our purpose, driving ourselves forward, becoming our best selves, extending that energy to the world around us, and passing these lessons onto those who need it. That's empowering! That is stepping into your power and stepping into the light.

Healing Our Lineage

When it comes to your boundaries- your feelings, thoughts, and the blocks that prevent you living by them may not be yours! You may be simply living with boundaries in the ways you inherited and were taught and shown.

After looking into the boundary issues that arise due to the influences and traumas from our own past lives, the next step in our healing journey is to look at those that came before — our ancestors, and how their attitudes, beliefs and behaviours around boundaries directly affects us.

When we really examine our fears about something, we can sometimes notice that the feelings of fear that we have, and experience are not based on our own experiences in this lifetime. The experiences and beliefs of our ancestors may affect us in different ways:

- Ancestral Contracts: The promises our ancestors made that are still active right now. So, if our ancestors made a promise of poverty because they'd been mistreated by wealthy people, we may be still affected by this promise.
- Ancestral Karma: This is the effects of our ancestors' choices, both positive and negative, may be taking place right now, through you. For example, if your ancestors have been aggressors in some way, you may be affected by their actions.

- Ancestral Beliefs: I've found this to be the most common way our ancestors affect us. Their beliefs about life, people, and the world they lived in are still active within our family. If our ancestors believed they couldn't set boundaries, we may find it difficult too.

"The deeds of an ancestor can create family karma that continues to influence the fate of the family's descendants until the karma is dissolved." - Dr Hiroshi Motoyama

Ancestral Healing

When we look and undertake ancestral healing, we are healing our lineage — those that came before us, ourselves, and those that follow us. Native Americans believe that we are affected by seven generations of our ancestors, both before and after us. The energetic wounds of the generations before us have been passed down to us. If you read further into ancestral healing, there's scientific proof of this phenomenon, called epigenetics. Even if we don't know our biological family their DNA and karmic energy lives within us - that connection is still made.

Now, you might be reading this and thinking that you don't know seven generations of your biological family's history, either because the stories of the people weren't passed down in your family, or, like many, you weren't raised by your biological parents. At this time, and for this healing, don't worry about that. We can spiritually connect with our lineage still and feel the effect of this work. We can also work with what we call our chosen family. If you are adopted or raised by stepparents, you are also influenced by them, and they can be included in our ancestral healing work. We can even look to include certain friends - those that are around us who have a strong, long-term influence on our lives.

This can seem like a huge undertaking - seven generations of family could easily amount to 200 people, living and past – but, simply put, we are trying to repair our stories and make changes where we feel they are needed. Ancestral healing helps us let go of the past, transmutes any energies that don't serve us, and helps us to learn the lessons that need to be learnt. The best way to heal and honour our ancestors is to live our lives aligned with our purpose.

Ancestral healing can be a deep and enlightening process. It can go as deep as you wish and help with challenging themes and issues in our lives, such as grief, shame, feelings of unworthiness, abuse, addiction, guilt, rejection and abandonment.

In the context of boundaries and for our work, like I've said, our ancestors' attitudes, beliefs and behaviours, and how they lived will have been passed down us.

Although I don't directly know the generations before me, from looking at both sides of my family, I could tell that this healing was going to make a difference. That can be true for many of us. Our healing starts with our living relatives and those close to us to whom we share strong connections with. Did we live in a home where the people around us growing up had poor or non-existent boundaries? Did we see examples of family members over giving, being scared of confrontation, or not standing up for themselves?

My parents, I would say, both have issues with boundaries. At times they are way too giving to others, neither valuing themselves (in my opinion) enough or in the way that I would like them to, and they have issues saying no to people when they really ought to for their own wellbeing. I was raised by pagan parents, who chose trusted people to share their beliefs with, and others they sheltered it from. I see many of their ways and traits in myself — and this is, of course, natural.

We don't grow up in a vacuum. When we are raised by people, we are raised with their behaviours around us all the time. We watch and our influenced by them, and they teach us how to be. If we are raised believing that to get on in life we must give, give, give, or hide much of ourselves away, then of course this will be at the core of our beliefs and issues.

But, from this work, I know and acknowledge that they are doing their best — my parents did and do what they feel is right — because they too are influenced by their lineage. We all are. We are bought up by our parents, who were bought up by their own parents, and so on. We unconsciously inherit many of their beliefs and behaviours, going back generations. The people we are, to a great extent, are who we are taught to be with all the beliefs, wounds, and patterns that are passed down to us.

Change starts with us

So, we head back into our journal for our first step on this journey, thinking about how we deal with our world when it comes to boundaries. You might want to refer back to the notes that you made back in the previous chapters. Ask yourself and free write about how much of how you react to situations in life where boundaries are needed, or set and crossed by others, is how your parents' behaviour was? You may wish to also think about other relatives and very close friends who have had an immediate effect on your life, and you've spent a lot of time with. What are the lessons you are learning here?

When we look back at these notes, we can most likely see patterns that we know we repeat ourselves. Again, we're highlighting where our behaviours come from, but also taking responsibility and control of the change we're going to gift ourselves, and the generations that follow us. Take some time to acknowledge at this point that our parents, or other people we've written about, were most likely doing their best. Ultimately, just like us, they are following what they were taught, behaviour in ways they were shown, and living out the ways that were passed down to them. It's an important step to acknowledge this for them, and for ourselves.

If you feel called to at this time, I find it helpful to practice a simple forgiveness ritual. This healing can release resentments and forgiveness. It's also important to let go of judgements. So, simply close your eyes and, as you call each situation and person to mind, send a loving energy to them. If you're a visual person, this could be a pink or white light, or simply breathing and feel the energy of love and forgiveness being sent from your heart to theirs.

Finally, we cut the cords with the behavioural patterns around boundaries that have been passed to us. In this step we are acknowledging that these are our old patterns - and we are stepping away from them now. We covered cutting cords previously and now is a great time to revisit this and cut and transmute these cords.

Remember, all these rituals, practices and alike can be repeated as often as you wish.

Whether you wish to talk to your living relatives about this healing is of course up to you. You may feel that the above practice is enough for you, you may want to have conversations with people and know that they will find it helpful and be receptive to your thoughts, or you may feel that by gently changing your own behaviours they will come to see and learn from you. We know the people around us best, so I leave any possible interactions up to you and your intuition to guide you on.

Healing with our ancestors

As I mentioned, many of us do not know our family tree going back many generations. You might be lucky and have an interest in genealogy or know a family member that has researched this and shared stories with you. Either way, we can still work with our ancestors and healing patterns of behaviours that don't support our boundaries.

When I started this work, I found it comforting. To know that those immediately related to me shared issues with boundaries actually helped, in the sense that I wasn't alone. I'm still responsible for my problems, but I can see where my reactions and behaviours were influenced. To know that my family may have experienced these patterns over hundreds of years gone by was a weird thought to get my head around at first. I sadly didn't know my grandparents to literally test the theory that they had had boundary issues. So, it came down to trust. Trust that this went deeper, trust that this healing would bring shifts, trust that (as ever) I had been taken in this direction for a reason. I'm going to share with you two simple rituals, but first a few things to note:

- If you don't know the name of the ancestor, you can use their relationship to you to call them in - for instance my great grandmother on my mother's side.
- Rituals are a great way to connect with ancestors.
- We need to ask our ancestors to work with us. You can simply ask 'please support me" or "thank you for working with me…"
- You can connect through prayer, meditation, free

writing, songs and chants, leaving offerings on an altar or sacred space you set for them.

Ancestors and Connection Ritual

This ritual helps you connect with your ancestors and receive answers and guidance to any questions you have. We can, for example, simply ask for their help as we move towards having healthy boundaries in our lives. We can also ask what more we can do, or where we might need to set new boundary that we may not be aware of yet.

- *The first step with any ritual is to plan, plan, plan! What do you feel called to include? Photos of family members; any personal items of theirs you may have; an offering to them - something like flowers, a glass of wine, or food are often suggested as offerings to make; candles; and divination tools that you are familiar with and use like oracle or tarot cards, or a pendulum. What questions do you have or what support do you want to ask for when it comes to your boundaries and the work you are doing? Arrange a time when you can work with this ritual and be totally undisturbed. I find around an hour is a good length of time to have available.*

- *Prepare yourself - clear and protect your energy, using sage, a bubble of light or any other methods you are comfortable with, and ground yourself.*

- *Set an intention, prayer or visualise how you want the ritual to go - and that it is for the highest good of you and your ancestral lineage.*

- *Light your candle and spend at least a few moments in meditation, quietening your mind. Set the intention to connect with your ancestors. Maybe one in particular, or just any who are able to help you with your boundaries.*

- *Ask any questions you have and see what answers you receive. Free write the messages that come through, any feelings you experience etc. If you want to pull any cards or similar this is a great time to do so.*

- *Send forgiveness if appropriate to those that have come forward for you. You can use a simple mantra - "Thank you for my lesson, I love you, I forgive you".*

- *Give thanks and send gratitude to your ancestors for being here with you and working with you during this ritual.*

- *Close the ritual - place your offering in your space. Blow out the candle.*

- *Shift your energy - cut any cords, move your body, get outside in nature, ground yourself, cleanse in a salt bath.*

The more you do this ritual, the more naturally it will come and the more intuitive it will be. Many feel called to do this at times where the veil is thinnest - Samhain for instance - as the connection can come more easily at this time. As with anything, feel when and how you are called to and are most comfortable to do this ritual.

Family Tree Healing Ritual

This is a gentle ritual that sends loving healing to the whole of your family tree - those you know and identify with and those still to come. When we are healing our boundary issues - or any healing - we do not heal alone.

It is said that the best time to do this ritual is on a full moon. You'll need to gather a few things in preparation - a candle, a crystal (something like ancestralite, flint, rose quartz, quartz, Eye of the Storm (Judy's Jasper), and an image representing a family tree image (with or without names). I use a drawn image of a tree showing all of the branches and roots deep within the ground. The branches represent the present and future generations, the roots represent our ancestors.

- *Prepare yourself - clear and protect your energy, using sage, a bubble of light or any other methods you are comfortable with, and ground yourself.*

- *Set an intention, prayer or visualise how you want the ritual to go - and that it is for the highest good of you and your ancestral lineage.*

- *Light your candle and spend at least a few moments in meditation, quietening your mind.*

- *Ensure your crystal is cleansed, charged and an appropriate healing intention set.*

- *Place the crystal at the bottom of the deepest root of the tree in the image. Set the intention that this is the place of healing boundaries for the whole family.*

- *Sit with the image and feel/visualise the crystal sending forgiveness and loving compassion up the tree, through all the roots, trunk and branches, and reprogramming any negative patterns as it goes.*

- *Visualise that love out into the branches and leaves that haven't grown yet - for the benefit of future generations.*

- *Visualise the crystal seeding gifts for future generations.*

- *Visualise that love and healing travelling into your own heart.*

- *Should you wish to you can add further crystals at*

points on the image you feel called for (like a crystal grid).

- *Finish the ritual by blowing out the candle and leave the crystal(s) in place overnight in the light of the full moon.*

- *The following morning remove and cleanse all the crystals.*

As the change maker in your family, the healing sent to your lineage during these rituals and work is incredibly powerful. You are working towards a better future for yourself and the generations that come after you - as well as honouring your ancestors for all they gave to you.

"Pain travels through family lines until someone is ready to heal it in themselves. By going through the healing, you no longer pass the poison chalice onto the generations that follow. It's incredibly important and sacred work." - Stephi Wagner

Forgiveness and Grounding

All of this healing and the work we are undertaking can bring up and release resentments, judgements, and outdated perceptions — and forgiveness is an important part of our process. For me, forgiveness and healthy boundaries go hand in hand.

When I say forgiveness, I'm not talking about personally contacting and offering forgiveness to everyone who has ever crossed those boundary lines or disrespected you, and in doing so giving them permission to do the same again. When you do put healthy boundaries in place some people will see their past behaviour and change, and for them forgiveness is appropriate. But this exercise is a personal ritual primarily focused on our internal focus and forgiving ourselves, and the important step and healing this brings us.

All I had learnt about my boundaries, the way I'd lived before, and of course the accident that was the turning point all had one thing in common: I had reached a point where I needed to move forward and on from them all. I needed to forgive. I had to forgive myself — past me and present me — for my actions. For not saying no, and for not knowing or doing better. I had to forgive those people around me who had crossed my boundaries previously (knowing so or otherwise).

I had to forgive as it felt like this allowed me to wipe the slate clean. Forgiving and grounding myself in the present seemed like those natural final pieces in the jigsaw puzzle that had been my journey. If I could do both of these, then I could move my life forward — step into my new power.

"Forgiveness gives me boundaries because it unhooks me from the hurtful person, and then I can act responsibly, wisely. If I am not forgiving them, I am still in a destructive relationship with them." — Henry Cloud

Ho'oponopono

Ho'oponopono is a beautiful Hawaiian practice for forgiveness. I am definitely someone who has struggled with forgiveness, and the concept of 'forgive and forget'. I find Ho'oponopono to be both comforting and a beautiful mantra to recite, and a loving way to approach forgiveness.

According to the Hawaiian practices, we have a spiritual body, mental body and an emotional body that are all a part of our physical body. The art of Ho'oponopono is where it connects our mind and body, and sends healing out into the world, healing through forgiveness.

The mantra – *'I'm sorry, Please forgive me, Thank you, I love you'* - has 4 elements to it. They involve the power of Repentance, Forgiveness, Gratitude and Love.

I'm sorry - Repentance - With this step, the tradition holds that we are responsible for everything that is in our mind. I like this when it comes to boundaries. Like I've said in previous chapters, so much of what had blocked me were my thoughts and perceptions, my fears and my ego. Once I realised and worked through that, it felt very natural and fitting to say I'm sorry and to accept responsibility. I am sorry - to myself for not fully honouring my authenticity, to those I projected my feelings on to, and to my boundaries for not honouring them. In so many ways, I'm sorry. Traditionally with this apology we are saying *"I realise that I am responsible for the issues with my boundaries in my life and I feel terrible remorse that something in my consciousness has caused this."*

Please forgive me - Forgiveness - Don't worry about who we're asking. Just ask! Please forgive me. Say it over and over. Mean it. Feel it. Remember what the *I'm sorry* meant, as we ask to be forgiven. During this step I forgive myself and those that have crossed my boundaries — past, present, and I also send it into the future too.

Thank you - Gratitude - Again with this step, it doesn't really matter who you are thanking; just the step, action and energy of being thankful. You don't even have to be specific (unlike with a more traditional gratitude practice) about what you are thankful for. Just say thank you. To yourself, to the universe, to whoever you believe in- just say thank you, thank you, thank you! If I do want to be specific to my boundaries, I thank myself for the work that I've done. I thank the people in my life who taught me lessons about boundaries. I thank the universe for always holding me, and those that love me for being there for me throughout this journey.

I love you - Love - There is nothing more powerful than the energy of love. Say I love you. Say it to yourself, to those around you, to everyone and everything. Say I love you to your boundaries, to your challenges, to yourself. Say it over and over again: I love you!

With each step in the tradition of Ho'oponopono, the important things are to feel each part, say it as many times as you feel called to, and mean it. Embody and feel each word and sentiment. It can feel strange at first, but it's a beautiful tool and practice, and you'll know when it clicks for you. For me, it felt like it softened me, it opened my heart, it made me feel accepting of myself and others, events and situations, and it helped all my healing fall into place.

Close your eyes and as you call each situation where your boundaries were crossed, and the people involved to mind, recite the Ho'oponopono mantra - "I'm sorry, please forgive me, Thank you, I love you." You can say it out loud, or in your head. However, you are most comfortable.

By practicing Ho'oponopono you are giving yourself a clean

slate when it comes to any boundary issues in the past - and allowing yourself to move on free of any burdens your issues with boundaries have bought into your life.

As you move forward, the next and the final step in our healing work, is to ground ourselves. We have addressed and worked through so much- we have forgiven, and our slate is now clean. Now we ground our energy.

Grounding

Grounding is a common and essential spiritual practice. Grounding keeps our energy stable and keeps us in touch with and connected to the energies of the Earth. If we aren't grounded, we can feel 'floaty' and it makes focusing on and dealing with our day to day life and tasks difficult. When we ground ourselves, we connect our energy with that of the Earth, or Mother Earth, and we draw any excess energy we may have in our body and chakras down through our feet to be stabilised in the ground.

When it comes to our boundaries, being grounded will support us, helping us manage any anxieties that come up as we start to live by all we have learnt.

If our energy isn't grounded, it can lead to anxieties. These anxieties can make us feel unable to live by our boundaries and may lead us to go back to our old habits and behaviour patterns — just like those we've covered - as these are more known to us and may therefore seem more comfortable and easier. As well as the spiritual perspective, many counsellors recommend grounding as a self-soothing tool to use when we are having a bad day or dealing with a lot of stress, overwhelming feelings, and/or anxiety. A perfect tool therefore to add to our boundary journey.

As we start to facilitate our new ways of being, staying grounded is essential. It will help integrate our spiritual and our physical energy and help us take steps to care for the new ways and mindset that we have. When we ground, we balance our energy - it is equally distributed through our body and chakras and that balance is key to being aware of your boundaries, making your ability to enforce them and live by them all the more powerful.

Grounding is a simple practice — you can either visualise roots coming from the bottom of your feet, going down into the earth, through the layers of soil, rocks and such until these roots reach the centre of the earth, where they find a large quartz crystal and wrap themselves round it. That's my favourite way to ground.

You can also walk barefoot on grass, or on a beach if you're lucky enough to have one close to you. You can also eat a small amount of dark chocolate (another favourite). If you simply cannot get outside and would like to ground, you can sit with a piece of black tourmaline between your feet. Sitting with this while taking deep breaths is an incredibly grounding practice.

Make grounding part of your daily spiritual practice. It will support you in this work, and so much more.

Part Three: Stepping into Your Power

Living by Your Boundaries

For the time in which we've not honoured our boundaries, we have effectively dis-empowered ourselves. Now, as we start to put into place this new way of living by our boundaries, we take back that power. It takes courage to be honest with people, and to enforce the lines we know we need to draw. You may also notice that as you become empowered by taking this action for yourself that you want to see more change and growth in other areas of your life.

When we work through the healing, we get to a point where everything we now have and know comes into practice. We have to step out into the world with our new expectations and values of ourselves and for our life. This is what our boundaries give us. Living by our boundaries means that we are going to start changing patterns. We're going to start living in an authentic way, looking after and valuing ourselves above others.

Communication and Throat-Chakra Clearing

As I mentioned, clear, honest, and authentic communication is key to living by healthy boundaries. We need to be able to speak up for ourselves and to communicate clearly. With the care we know as spiritually minded people, we want to impart on the world and those around us.

Being clear about our boundaries and communicating this to others is vital. Remember, most people aren't overstepping our boundaries on purpose – they're simply responding to how we've acted previously, our energetic vibration and the standards that we've set for ourselves.

Saying *no* can take a lot of adjustment. It's going to feel strange at first and can be hard for people around us to accept – especially if we've been a *yes* person for a long time. The best thing you can do if you find yourself wanting to say no, is to be honest with yourself and the other person by just saying no.

Keeping your throat chakra clear and removing any blocks of energy will help when you start to feel like those words aren't coming easily.

There are simple ways to help keep your throat chakra clear. If you are attuned to reiki or any other healing modality, you can of course use this. If you're not attuned, then I believe you still have this healing energy within you. Simply place one hand gently over your throat and breathe deeply. When you feel calm, start to send your breath to the area your hand is placed on, as you do so you can also visualise the colour blue.

You can also wear the colour blue, wear or carry blue crystals, such as lapis lazuli, turquoise, aquamarine, and celestite.

You can also use these simple affirmations to help .... 'It's easy for me to share my boundaries with others', 'It's safe for me to share my boundaries with others'.

The practical, muggle life bit

Although this is a spiritual book, with woo-woo healing at the core and essence, I wouldn't leave you without some more practical tips to help all the amazing work you have done fall into place in the world and situations we are living in.

Whether you are dealing with friends, family, work colleagues, or clients in your own spiritual or healing business, I know that some of the examples below will resonate. I'm sure you'll read them and be able to put names and faces from your day-to-day life by the scenarios:

So, do you have a friend who is constantly late? They rarely show up on time to anything, leave you waiting alone and generally this habit frustrates and angers you. Perhaps you've even started to not want to keep dates and arrangements with them because you're really annoyed with this situation. Well, there's a boundary to communicate here - the boundary perhaps is that you kindly let them know that if they're going to be more than 10 minutes late, they need to text you and let you know. That way you, for example, don't have to rush after work or have more time to finish a task before you meet them. So, you can say and put that to them... *"Hey, if you're going to be late, to save me rushing, can you please just let me know"*.

Do you have someone who calls on you just to emotionally dump on you? They seem to do nothing but constantly tell you all about their bad day, bad situation etc. We're empaths, so I'm guessing you do! Remember that it's ok if you're not in a place to deal with that call today to just say, *"I'm really sorry, I'm feeling drained today."* Or *"I'm not feeling great myself today* (insert whatever the situation is for you) *and I can't really talk right now. Can I give you a call in the week?"* And then call when you do have the energy, time, and headspace to deal with that call. It's ok to not be 100% available to everyone all of the time.

And here's some simple sentences for various situations:

- I can't do that, but I can help you find someone who can.
- I appreciate the gesture, but in the future, would you mind....

- I can't take on additional responsibilities right now.
- I'm not comfortable discussing that topic with you.
- Thanks for your concern, but I can handle this.
- I can't attend, but I appreciate the invitation. Thank you.
- I can't do <x>, but I could do <y>.
- I'm allowed to change my mind.
- No, thank you.

Maybe even, because you know your life and the scenarios that you may face and resonate with you the most, you can write yourself some little scripts like the above and keep them to hand. That way you've lived out the conversation the way you would like it to go once already. You have the time to think and put it a way that you are comfortable and feel confident with and you have that useful tool to hand.

I hope from these examples you can practically see how putting these little boundaries can work. I know that, with all the work and healing, it may still feel uncomfortable at first because we're pushing out of our comfort zone — but it's not impossible. It can be gentle not rude, but really, we are honouring ourselves, protecting our mindset, our energy, and how we feel.

I am someone who firmly believes that every healing journey is an onion, and we just keep peeling layers off, revealing more and doing the work. I am a proud onion peeler! I also found that along with my cards, crystals, meditations and alike the following practical steps help:

Schedule alone time — start with 30 minutes a week and build up to what feels healthiest for you. Put it in your diary and stick to it. Use this time rest and recharge. Do something that helps you unwind and gives you the headspace to reflect on what's going on in life, how you're feeling, and what you want to do next.

Journalling - a useful tool to help you reflect and help you identify where and what boundaries you may need to put into place, communicate or strengthen. Grab a pen and free write everything down. Make it a huge brain dump of thoughts and feelings and then work through to see patterns that you can then work and improve on.

At work — don't take on more than you can handle because you feel under pressure to do so. Taking on more than you can sensibly manage leads to stress and gives your boss and others unrealistic expectations that you will feel pressured to live up to. Instead, chat to your boss honestly and openly about what you can take on, and how you see projects and tasks working best for you and them.

Turn off your phone and the media (including social media) - being connected 24 hours a day, seven days a week, isn't good for anyone. You have to have space from the unrealistic images of other people's lives on social media, and the negativity that come through these channels and the more traditional media. If you want some time out to relax and watch TV in the evening, make it something that makes you laugh and feel good. Unfollow or mute social media accounts or people that negatively impact you.

Take care of your body - the old saying of "*take care of your body and it will take care of you*" really is true! Eat good, healthy, nourishing foods and drink plenty of water. And you know what - a little of something that you fancy is good too I say! Worked hard all week and fancy that chocolate treat? Then don't deprive yourself if it's all in balance and moderation. (I once found my doctor with a McDonalds breakfast wrapper in his bin! Even he was ok with that as a treat at the end of long week). Create a healthy sleep routine and a positive morning routine.

Say yes only when you truly mean it - don't answer people's requests or asks for favours, with a yes immediately unless that is a from the gut with an intuitive, heartfelt YES! If it's a maybe yes, or a I don't want to say yes but I'll have to, then ask for time to think about it and tell them you will come back to them. Think it through and then give them their answer. After some thought, that yes may come easier and be a more affirmative, positive yes. Or it could actually be a firm no, and that's ok. Better to explain it's no and why, then say yes and resent it.

Remember that it's ok to say I can't do this right now, can I come back to you? And other workarounds and kind ways to give yourself space from the people or situations that drain you.

Understand the environments, atmospheres and situations that trigger you - the more you are aware of your triggers, the more you can learn how to work around these - and work on getting comfortable with communicating these and suggesting ways to see people in alternate environments.

Healing therapies like acupuncture, reflexology, sound baths, creative activities (drawing, painting, dancing etc.) all re-energise spiritually minded people.

And please... never forget to love yourself and acknowledge your achievements.

Closing ritual - honour how far you've come

I mentioned early on in the book that at this point we would spend some time honouring our journey with a closing ritual.

Now this ritual isn't to say this work is done or to finalise it in any way. As you'll know by now, I firmly believe we never stop healing. You can revisit this book as often as you need, if you find your boundaries being crossed or feeling like you are being pushed to. I also believe, however, that when you make progress on any growth journey you should honour that- acknowledge and celebrate the work that you've put in, and the time and commitment that you've made to yourself.

If you look back to how you felt about boundaries and situations in your own life when you started this journey and where you are now, how does that make you feel?

Please take some time, light a candle, and spend a few moments quietly thinking about how far you've come. You are amazing. I see you and I see that. Honour yourself in this moment.

When you're ready announce to the universe and set the intention - "I am now going to live by my sacred boundaries".

The Spiritual Toolkit for Sacred Boundaries

This chapter is actually how the idea for this whole book came about. I came to realise how much my spiritual tools supported my process in keeping healthy boundaries in place. Whether that would be a crystal I would carry to help give me that extra strength, or the cards I would pull to dig deeper.

Although a light workers journey with their boundaries can be really difficult, I'm in awe of the tools that we have to help us that our 'muggle 'friends simply don't understand. The following pages are the tools that I want to share with you that regularly excite and amaze me, and that I come to rely on for whatever stage my boundary journey is currently at - because this journey doesn't end. Apologies if you thought, *"Hey, I'm most of the way through this book so I'm almost done."*

We will change and grow, and our boundaries will shift at different times in our lives. We will experience periods where we waiver and periods where it takes us more energy to stand strong. Remember the onion and the layers that you just keep peeling away? Working with your boundaries is the same.

But these tools and all the healing you've done so far will help. You can revisit any chapter and any of the healings at any point you feel called to.

You can also dip in and out of the tools below. These are here to support you, to bring a little extra magic to this journey.

Working with cards:

Sometimes where we feel as though the lack with our boundaries and the journey becomes difficult to understand or get to grips with, we can need a nudge to help us identify blocks and our next steps.

The following card spreads are suitable to use with angel, oracle or tarot cards, and any deck you feel drawn to.

Knowing your blocks spread:

This five-card spread is an amazing tool for identifying what we need to know about any particular block. Think of a situation, and shuffle your cards while setting the intention of receiving the guidance you need:

Card 1: What is the root cause of the block in this situation?

Card 2: What fear inside you is this situation bringing to the fore?

Card 3: What is the energetic effect overall on your life being blocked by this situation?

Card 4: What is the healing work you are being guided to carry out to help you?

Card 5: What are the next steps and practical action to take to help you move forward?

Setting boundaries spread:

This four-card spread provides guidance on how to deal with particular people who may be pushing, or crossing your boundaries:

Card 1: Who asks too much of you?

Card 2: How could you respond to them next time?

Card 3: What would help you clearly communicate your boundaries to them?

Card 4: What will give you strength when dealing with them?

Crystals for boundaries:

I love to work with crystals. It may be my favourite of all my tools and healing, supportive practices. They're energy and beauty never fail to amaze me. So, it will come as no surprise that crystals played a part in my boundary journey.

If you've not worked with crystals, you can find my Crystal Magic 101 over on my website (*www.sacredmoon.me*) to find out how to get started.

Whether you want to pop a crystal in your pocket for extra support, meditate with it for clarity, use it for healing, or have it in your space to help with strength or protection, these are the crystals I'm going to personally recommend that can help you as you take on this healing and to protect your boundaries in future:

Amazonite: When it comes to boundaries Amazonite helps us identify and set personal boundaries, supporting us to see clearing how we want our relationships to be, and give us the self-discipline to enforce our boundaries and not be tempted to waiver.

Black Tourmaline: During our boundary journey, we will be aware of the negativity people around us, as well as blocks and negative thoughts that we are personally working through. Black Tourmaline blocks and repels negative energy and will help keep us clear and protected while we are on our journey.

Black Obsidian: At times when we found our boundaries tested or that we feel people around us are pushing our boundaries, Black Obsidian will support us through challenging situations and to preserve with the work towards our goals.

Blue Kyanite: Linked to the energy of Archangel Michael, Kyanite can help with cutting cords, maintaining boundaries and communicating our needs clearly while holding our own.

Cherry Orchard Jasper: A more little known crystal, sometimes also called Septinite, it teaches us to set boundaries, say no to difficult situations and helps us get comfortable with saying no without feeling fear and/or guilt when doing so. It's one of my favourites for this work and if I had to recommend just one off this list, it would be this crystal.

Hematite: When we are working with energetic and emotional boundaries, Hematite helps support our work. It also absorbs negative energy, like stress and anxiety, and can be a powerful crystal to use when we are overcoming our fears around boundaries.

Rhodonite: Not only will Rhodonite help with heart healing and encourage you to treat yourself with compassion during this journey, but it will also support you in detaching from the expectations of others and supports your boundaries.

Crystal grid for boundaries:

Crystal grids bring together the powerful vibrations of crystals to all work together to assist with one intention. In a grid your crystals basically work as team, focussed on helping what you've asked for assistance with.

If you are someone who likes to work with crystal grids, or would like to try your first grid, this is my go-to recommendation for a simple crystal grid to support you and this work as you embark on this journey.

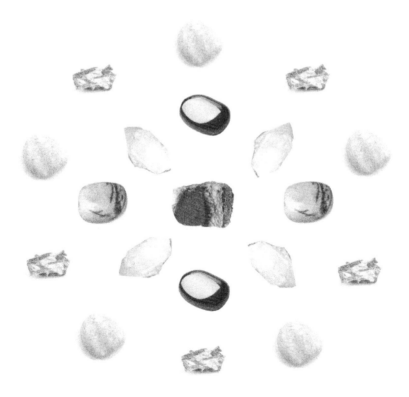

This grid will support your new mindset and help facilitate the healing you need:

- Centre stone - Cherry Orchard Jasper (for guilt free, healthy boundaries)

- Around the centre stone - Clear Quartz points (the master healer crystal helps direct and magnify the energy of the grid)

- First circle - alternating rhodonite and hematite (for healing and support, and overcoming our fears)

- Second circle - alternating amazonite and blue kyanite (for setting and communicating boundaries).

First thing to do for a grid is find a space where it can sit, undisturbed. Write your intention for your boundaries on a piece of paper and fold it up. Your centre crystal (or all your crystals) will sit on this paper.

Then cleanse your crystals and program them to work with you. You're now ready to place your crystals in the grid!

Once your grid is in place, activate it with you intention. So, whilst your sat or stood with your grid, speak your intention loudly putting it out into the universe. You can say something like *"I set this grid to support my healing and to help me communicate my boundaries to those around me"*, or whatever resonates and feels most suited to you.

Essential oils for boundaries:

Add a few drops of any of these oils to a diffuser or to bath water to help on days you are finding boundaries difficult to maintain:

Rosemary keeps you strong in your boundaries so that you do not lose yourself in other people. Rosemary helps you understand your value and feel self-reliant. When you know deep down what you're worth, it's much easier to enforce and maintain boundaries with confidence.

Basil helps clear negativity and with feelings of fatigue. Using basil on a regular basis will help you build trust with yourself so that you can honour your needs and stay open-hearted in the process.

Melaleuca (also known as Tea Tree oil) is known as the oil of energetic boundaries. It can clear negative energetic baggage caused by individual relationships. It helps to break the negative ties in relationships so that healthy boundaries can be formed.

Calling back our power:

If at any time we feel drained by enforcing our boundaries, or feel like it's too hard, or that we're overwhelmed, we may well need to call back our power.

As we go about our lives, we can leave our energy - both positive and negative - out in the world, and of course we are absorbing positive and negative energies as we go about our day to day lives. I use this little prayer, influenced by a ritual of Gabby Bernstein's, to both cleanse my energy and call back any energies to me.

Thank you, angels and guides of the highest truth and compassion, for removing any negative energy that I may have picked up today and retrieving any positive energy I may have lost.

I repeat this daily at the end of each day, as part of my spiritual practice, and at any other time I'm feeling really drained and I can't quite identify why.

Affirmations:

Affirmations are positive statements that can help you to challenge and overcome self-sabotaging and negative thoughts. When you repeat them often and believe in them, you can start to make positive changes. These affirmations are written to help and support your boundary journey:

- I honour myself by honouring my boundaries.
- I am expressing myself clearly, kindly and fearlessly.
- I am worthy and deserving of maintaining boundaries

that serve me.

- Each and every day I'm becoming clearer and clearer about the boundaries that serve me best.
- My boundaries help me take loving care of my body, mind and soul each any every day, in each and every way.

Boundaries and planetary energy:

In astrology, each planet relates to and represents a different set of qualities and characteristics, and rule over a different part of our lives. I believe that during certain times we can work with this energy to support our boundaries and this journey:

Moon Ritual

No doubt you will have heard about the magic of working with the moon, may have heard of *Moonology* by teacher and author Yasmin Boland, and maybe you already work with the lunar cycle to set intentions and release feelings, habits and alike.

I've always told friends that don't hold spiritual beliefs or work with moon's energy, that they can look at it from the woo-woo perspective, or simply see it as a regular way of checking in with their goals, how their life is working for them and what's bothering them or that they're holding onto unnecessarily.

Your boundary journey also has its place for reflection and a check in during the lunar cycle, helping to keep you on your path and doing any work that becomes needed.

The moon's cycle has eight phases - starting with the new moon where we plant seeds of our dreams and set intentions, into the waxing crescent phase where we further explore those dreams and commit to them in the first quarter and gibbous phases. We release and forgive in the full moon phase, and as the moon starts to disappear from our skies again, we start to regroup.

The last quarter phase, about 7-10 days after the full moon, is the time to give up bad habits and remove yourself from unhealthy situations. This is the phase of the moon cycle that is all around re-evaluating balance in our lives and trust. It's the perfect time to review how your boundaries are working for you, where you are keeping good healthy boundaries, where you may be being too firm and rigid, and where you need to clear communicate those boundary lines.

In the early days of your boundary journey and healing work, I recommend making note of when this last quarter phase falls. Mark out these three days and make a note in your diary to take some time - even just an hour or so - to just review how you're feeling with your boundaries, what situations have tried or tested those lines, how that felt, how you reacted, and what the last few weeks have bought to light for you.

Retrogrades:

A planetary retrograde is when a planet seems to be moving backwards in the sky from our perspective here on Earth. It's actually an optical illusion as planets don't actually move backwards! When it comes to astrology, ancient people realised that when a planet appears to change direction, the area of our lives that planet is said to rule will see challenges or confusion during that specific time. So, here's are some particular retrogrades to watch for and that can make our boundaries challenging or confusing...

Mercury Retrograde

Mercury Retrograde also comes around 2-3 times a year. Many feel that this is a scary time thanks to the thousands of memes on the internet blaming Mercury being retrograde for life's problems.

Mercury Retrograde is a time when the energy supports us to evaluate how we communicate and how we are actively present with our lives.

So, as well as backing up my technology and being super careful with what and how I type emails and texts, I use this time to again just review where I am with my boundaries and how I'm letting people clearly and kindly know where I am with situations and commitments. This is often a time where little things have crept up and come to light. Maybe I'm checking my emails late at night again - I seem to catch myself doing that a lot when this particular retrograde period creeps in - or I find a situation where I have held back or compromised a little further than I was totally comfortable with. And all of that is ok - these check in points that the planets provide us with are here to help us.

Venus Retrograde

At points where Venus' path goes retrograde, we can see people who have previously pushed our boundaries, not respected them and crossed the lines with us reappear. It's a time where this issues with individuals, or the individual themselves, can raise their head again and reappear in our lives. On a positive, it gives us the opportunity to heal those relationships and heal within us the deeper hurt or trauma behind that experience, as well as the situation and issue with that person.

Mars Retrograde

Mars' path going retrograde gives us the opportunity to tackle issues once and for all. Having boundaries where you need to be really firm, no nonsense, and be really clear about them can be easier with this energy behind and supporting us. It's also a time that highlights self-care too - so looking after yourself while you do any tough boundary work is really vital. It's a time where you can lay down firm boundaries, but only if they are related to a situation where you truly never want or need any flexibility. This time is really for the boundaries where we can never take them back. So, if you see that Mars is retrograde while you're on this journey, perhaps just put the book down until this time has passed, then pick it back up (and do make sure you pick it back up) and start again at a later date.

Life Now

Writing this book has been such a cathartic healing journey for me. It's shown me new wounds I hadn't acknowledged, traumas I thought I'd processed, and many little bits in between. It's shown me that I am someone willing to do the work. Always. That's all I want for each person who picks up this book — try and do the work. Because our journey is not yet written, and the more we do, the more we receive from the universe and grow in this lifetime.

Writing it has also made me so full of gratitude. Sometimes it's hard to know how that girl I once was got to be here in this present moment, tapping away on a keyboard and willing to share with the world. I am grateful for the journey, all it bought me and taught me, and how maybe it can help another person.

My life with a good set of healthy boundaries looks very different to what I experienced before. I'm not going tell you that I have this all down now, am absolutely perfect and never waver. I'm still healing. I still drive past lorries and wince for a start! Even recently I reached out to someone who had really betrayed me because a social situation had been so awkward, and I had a few words with myself the next day for taking it too far. There are still some people who I won't talk very openly about my spiritual journey. In some cases, there's still some fear there for me, and with some I know at this point in their life, they're not open to seeing or understanding it. I have every respect for that, and I know that's their thing and I can't and don't try to fix or change that. But it saddens me a little to have a whole area of like that I don't discuss with them. It leaves some conversations very stunted.

Lockdown was a struggle for me. Not so much the staying home aspect- for, as many empaths are, I'm happiest at home! But coming back out into the world tested all my boundaries again. I'd gotten too comfortable in lockdown, to be honest with you. It gave me all the permissions the world could give me to not see people, not to have those awkward conversations with people, and not be around draining people. But what lockdown took away from me was the balance I'd been working so hard to achieve, and that is so important with our boundaries. We have to have that balance of having people around us and going about our lives in the way that we want for our boundaries to be healthy. Our boundaries are never to shut the whole world out just to make discerning of who and what receives our energy. I was too happy hidden away, and coming back out into the world felt like restarting this journey again. And of course, being the happy empath in lockdown did get some strange reactions from those who felt like they were missing their life.

I accept help now......and I even ask for it! Because I recognise and truly believe that allowing those that support me to help me is not showing weakness. That was a huge shift for me! I am now more ok with being vulnerable.

One thing I am so careful of now is to honour myself and my time. Within my day job I no longer over commit to things that I know aren't feasible or are honestly above what I can deliver. I always try my best - and I know my best is all I can do, and it is good enough. In my business, I have times and days I work with my clients, and I have the balance of times when I will say, *"No, I want a day to myself."*

Recovering from my people pleasing ways and having a smaller inner circle have been perhaps the hardest two things and the things I dwell on at times. With friends, a lot has happened. People have come, people have gone. I allow myself time to grieve the people who either I can't have as close as they suck the energy from me, or the people who don't understand who I am and chose to leave themselves. This taught me a lot - mainly the distinction between the people who truly respect and value me, and those who don't. It's not been easy, but it created space and time in my life for people to come in who have become close friends who I can rely on and love hanging out with. And you know what — because of the balance I now have, and the fact that I am no longer being drained and overwhelmed by the life I was living, I have the time and energy to hang out with these friends! What I've learnt is that my boundaries don't mean the right people leave your life, they mean the space is made for the right people to be in your life!

This journey took years, so don't worry if you've come to the end of this little book of mine and you don't yet feel different. Just keep going. Honour yourself every day and everything will align.

I still work on my boundaries. I still have days where I need an affirmation, grab a crystal for some extra support, and take a little step back to my old ways. But I catch myself doing it, and I revisit what I need to. It's like any other part of our healing journey. Each layer of the onion sometimes brings a tear or two.

There's also been a lot of growth. By putting boundaries in place and working on my feelings around the expectations of others and how that was weighing so heavily on me, I've not only freed up time, but I also freed up mental space and my capacity to do and act on things that my intuition and guidance were leading me to. Like this book!

Finally, remember that our boundaries won't be the same forever. Every time we level up, we change and grow, and we have to readjust our boundaries. Our boundaries will flex and grow like we do. What we once didn't want in our lives, we might be more open to or even want to do. And that's ok. This isn't a one rule forever thing. I like to remind myself of the three C's for my boundaries: clarity, communication, centred. When I'm clear, communicate and come back to centre, I always know I'm going to be ok.

I sincerely, with my whole being and soul, hope this book has helped you in the way these healing helped me. I hope you now feel about to set, live by and are empowered by having healthy boundaries in your life. I believe this book is part of my soul contract for this lifetime. To learn the lessons and share them.

I wrote this book as I couldn't find the book to help me when I needed it. I also knew I had friends who needed these pages. If I know people who need these messages, I'm sure you do too. I would love it if you gifted this book to a friend, or someone you know it will help. Send them a copy as a gift, and as a simple step to help spread this ripple of healing.

Remember, when we heal, we don't heal alone. So, thank you for being part of my healing journey. Spread the love of boundaries through your own healing work, the changes you make, and the positive ripple effect this has on the world.

Thank You

This whole book didn't come about without the support of some amazing people who I'm so grateful and fortunate to share my journey and life with.

To my hubby, my soul mate in this lifetime, lifetimes past, and lifetimes I know are yet to come. While the popular phrase is that *'behind every great man, there is a great woman',* I know now, thanks to you, that this works both ways. You always have my back and are there cheering me on. To the moon and back, forever.

To my parents, thank you for not raising a princess but a badass witch. Thank you for all your help, my foundation and education, and always supporting me on this journey.

To my amazing friends who messaged, supported, read drafts, gave me feedback, encouragement, and were part of this journey. Thank you for being my cheer squad. You each amaze me with your various gifts and strengths, whether you see them or not — I see them —and wherever we are in this world I thank you for your support and being here.

To Kyle Gray and my angel friends. You are a such a part of this story, a catalyst for my growth, and I'm so grateful. My prayers saved me, and I prayed because you showed me how to trust in those words.

To Katie Oman, for being my book coach, kicking my butt

and helping me get this done! Thank you so much. You truly helped me realise a dream.

And of course, Dexter and Binx. Thank you for the cuddles, the head bops, and helping me when I didn't want to write and just needed a moment to be.

Printed in Great Britain
by Amazon

86103328R00088